Paul

A Beginner's Guide

Paul
A Beginner's Guide

Morna D. Hooker

ONEWORLD

A Oneworld Book

First Published by Oneworld Publications as
Paul: A Short Introduction, 2003
First published in the Beginners Guide Series, 2008
Reprinted, 2018, 2020

A CIP record for this title is available
from the British Library

ISBN 978–1–85168–564–6
eISBN 978–1–78074–173–4

Typeset by Jayvee, Trivandrum, India
Cover design by Two Associates
Printed and bound in Great Britain by Clays Ltd., Elcograf S.p.A.

Oneworld Publications
10 Bloomsbury Street
London WC1B 3SR
England

Contents

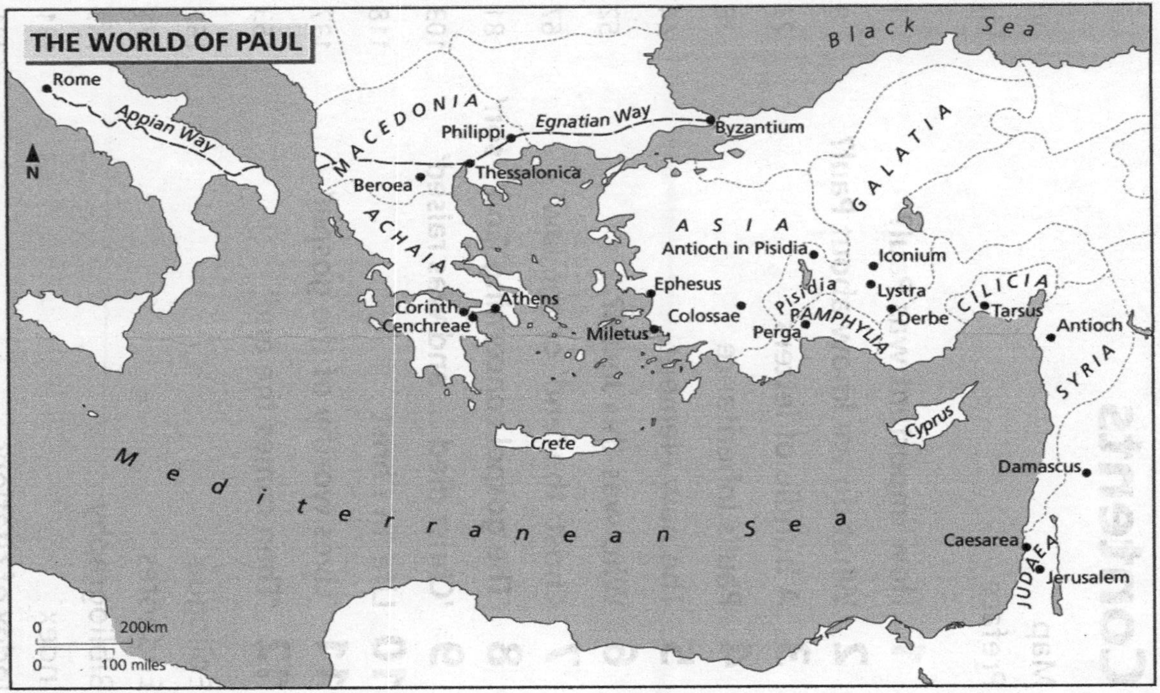
THE WORLD OF PAUL
Rome
Appian Way
N
MACEDONIA
Philippi
Egnatian Way
Byzantium
Thessalonica
Beroea
Black Sea
GALATIA
ACHAIA
ASIA
Antioch in Pisidia
Iconium
Ephesus
Pisidia
Lystra
CILICIA
Athens
Corinth
Cenchreae
Colossae
PAMPHYLIA
Derbe
Tarsus
Antioch
Miletus
Perga
SYRIA
Cyprus
Crete
Mediterranean Sea
Damascus
Caesarea
JUDAEA
Jerusalem
0 200km
0 100 miles

Preface

Many people find Paul difficult to comprehend. Some, in this age of political correctness, find him offensive. Those who attempt to understand him are sharply divided in their opinions: while some would agree with William Tyndale, who described Romans as the 'purest gospel', others dismiss Paul as the great perverter of the true religion of Jesus.

What is the truth? This book is based on the conviction that he is perhaps the most exciting theologian of all time, and certainly one of the most influential. The shape of Christian belief and the course of Christian history would have been very different without him. If we want to comprehend Christian thought, we need to wrestle with Paul's writings.

Attempting to understand Paul's thought is no easy matter, however. The challenge he presents is somewhat like that which would confront us if we were attempting to join together the pieces of a jigsaw, when many of the pieces were missing from the puzzle and there was no copy of the completed picture to guide us. We might well imagine features that were not there, and miss details that should be. Piecing together Paul's theology can be a frustrating task – but also a fascinating one. Grappling with what Paul really believed – and why he believed it – is well worth the struggle.

Paul's letters express his personal faith, and much of what he writes is written in the first person. In trying to explain what he means, I have frequently done the same, preferring to use 'we' and 'us' rather than employ ugly expressions such as 'humankind'.

Since much of what is written here depends on arguments that I have developed elsewhere, I have included indications as to where these more technical discussions can be found, for the benefit of those who may wish to examine them.

In referring to dates, I have preferred to use the conventional BC and AD, rather than BCE and CE. The latter terms were introduced in an attempt to be 'inclusive', but in fact exclude everyone except Jews and Christians! It seems better, when writing about a Christian theologian, to use a Christian calendar.

Finally, I would like to express my thanks to Anthony Bash, who both read the typescript through with a careful eye for problems, and encouraged me by his enthusiastic comments to complete it.

1

How important was Paul?

Two figures dominate the pages of the New Testament. The first is Jesus, the second, Paul. Although Paul himself would undoubtedly have protested that even to link his name with that of Jesus in this way was improper – since he was the 'slave of Christ', whose mission was to proclaim Jesus Christ as Lord – it is nevertheless true that Paul's influence on the development of what came to be known as 'Christianity' was immense. Thirteen of the twenty-seven documents that make up the New Testament claim to be written by him, and the larger part of the Acts of the Apostles is devoted to relating the story of Paul's missionary endeavours. Paul is the central figure in the New Testament between the middle of Acts and the end of Philemon.

Why was Paul so important? It is, in fact, worth reframing that question and asking whether he *was* as important *in his own lifetime* as we suppose. Or was his later influence due rather to the devotion of some of those who were close to him, and who carefully preserved his letters – perhaps even wrote, in his name, letters for the churches of the next generation, saying what they believed would have been his message for their particular situations? And since Paul is so clearly Luke's[1] 'missionary hero', the impression we gain from Acts – that the spread of the Christian gospel throughout the Mediterranean world was due almost entirely to Paul and his fellow-workers – may be a distorted one. What role did other Christians play in the spread of the gospel? How important a figure was Paul in the councils of the Church of his day? To many of his fellow-Christians, he seems to have been – to borrow Paul's own phrase – something of 'a thorn in the flesh'.[2] To the outside world, he was totally insignificant – except on those occasions when he was a nuisance to the authorities. And though he undoubtedly planted the Christian gospel in various strategic cities in the Roman world, the communities he formed were small, and largely ignored or abused by those around them.

Paul's legacy

Paul's legacy to later generations, however, was undoubtedly enormous, and he influenced the Church for all time. He is important, first, because his insistence that membership of God's people had been thrown open to Gentiles, and that the gospel must therefore be taken to them *without* demanding that they should become Jews in order to receive it, meant that what had begun as a Jewish sect became, within a few generations, a largely gentile movement; although Paul was not alone in taking up this position, he seems to have understood the issues involved more clearly than anyone else, and he certainly threw himself into the gentile mission without reserve. He is important, secondly, because the profound insights expressed in his epistles have fed and shaped Christian theology, spirituality and ethics ever since.

Paul's conviction that the gospel was intended for the Gentiles was not unique to him, and he was not alone in preaching to them. According to Galatians 2: 6–12, it is true, the leaders of the Jerusalem Church had recognized that Paul was called by God to be the apostle to the uncircumcised – though some Jewish Christians clearly disapproved (v. 12). But if Luke is to be believed, then even before Paul began his missionary work, there were moves in this direction. Luke tells us how Philip, one of the Greek-speaking members of the early Christian community, had preached the gospel to Samaritans and to an Ethiopian eunuch – someone who was not only not Jewish, but who (as a eunuch) was debarred from becoming a proselyte[3] – and had baptized them; his work in Samaria had been endorsed by Peter and John (Acts 8). Luke records, too, a tradition that Peter had been persuaded by a vision to visit Cornelius, a Gentile, and to preach the gospel to him; then, when the Holy Spirit descended on Cornelius, Peter realized that Gentiles might be baptized (Acts 10:1–11:18). When Paul himself began his mission work it was in Antioch (Acts 11:25–6), a city where the gospel had already been preached, not only to Jews but to Gentiles also (Acts 11:19–20).[4]

How reliable are these traditions? Scholars differ in the value they place upon them, but it seems reasonable to suppose that they reflect a development that was already taking place before Paul became a Christian. Paul may have been the apostle to the Gentiles *par excellence*, but he himself is aware that others were working in the same field (Rom. 1:13; 15:20). Indeed, the news that Christian Jews were mixing with Gentiles and worshipping with them may well have been one of the factors that led the pre-Christian Paul to persecute the Christian community with such vehemence.

Paul's second legacy is in his writings. But to what extent was the interpretation of the gospel expressed in Paul's epistles his own interpretation, and to what extent did he share it with other early Christians? In what ways did his beliefs overlap with theirs?

One of the reasons that it is so difficult to answer these questions is that Paul's letters are the earliest Christian documents to have come down to us. The accounts of Jesus' own teaching, the Gospels, were almost certainly written after Paul's death, and have been shaped by the needs and beliefs of those who passed on the tradition and wrote the Gospels. In the Acts of the Apostles, Luke tells us something of the early years of the Church, but there were no written records of what was said and done, and he is dependent on oral traditions. These were formative years, when men and women, reeling from recent events and trying to understand their significance, had not yet formulated their faith. We cannot assume that Luke's account of what the apostles said represents the way they expressed their beliefs at the time. Writing, as he does, with the benefit of hindsight, he is likely to assume that they understood then what in fact they came to grasp only later.[5]

Pre-Pauline tradition

In the absence of reliable accounts of what Christians *before* Paul had believed, scholars have turned to Paul's own letters in an attempt to discover 'pre-Pauline' tradition. Neat summaries of faith found in his writings are, they suggest, credal statements that were used in the early Christian communities, and which Paul has adopted and incorporated into his letters. There must, to be sure, have been ways of expressing Christian belief that would quickly become recognizable summaries: 'Jesus is Lord' is an obvious one – quoted both in Romans 10:9 and 1 Corinthians 12:3. Paul himself refers to 'the tradition' that he received, in 1 Corinthians 15:1ff, and this tradition consists of a summary statement of Jesus' death, burial, resurrection and appearances to various witnesses. Each of these summaries is quoted because it is relevant to the subject under discussion; the one quoted in 1 Corinthians is clearly adapted by Paul, who has added a reference to an appearance of the risen Christ to himself to the list of names included in the tradition.

Are there other such summaries of the gospel elsewhere? There are indeed – but are they Paul's *own* summaries, or did he 'inherit' them from other Christians? In favour of the latter, it is suggested, is the fact that these summaries are often 'rhythmic' in structure and sometimes employ 'unPauline vocabulary'. Unfortunately, in order to uncover the 'rhythmic structure', it is often necessary to delete certain phrases as 'Pauline additions'! In Romans 1:3–4, for example, we find this summary of the gospel concerning God's Son,

> who was descended from David according to the flesh
> and was declared to be Son of God [with power] according to
> the Spirit [of holiness by resurrection from the dead].[6]

If such credal summaries were indeed in circulation, we can understand why Paul might quote this couplet at the beginning of a letter written to a Christian community which does not know him, in order to establish that they share a common faith. If that was his intention, however, it would surely have served his purpose better if he had quoted the summary *without* any additions of his own! In fact, the whole passage may well have been written by Paul himself, since it is particularly appropriate as an introduction to the Epistle to the Romans, where Paul is going to discuss what is involved in life lived 'according to the flesh' and 'according to the Spirit' and the way in which, through Christ, Christians can move from one sphere to the other.

If the 'rhythmic structure' of these passages is not always obvious, neither is the 'unPauline' character of the vocabulary. The language of the summary in Romans 4:25, for example, which refers to Christians' belief in God,

> who raised Jesus our Lord from the dead –
> who was handed over to death for our trespasses
> and was raised for our 'justification',

sounds remarkably Pauline, though it is often assumed to be a traditional formula that he inherited. This time, the rhythmic structure is plain, and there are no 'additions' in need of excision. Are we to conclude that Paul's understanding of the gospel agreed exactly with that of those who were responsible for formulating this particular summary? Or that he wrote the summary himself?

At other times, the vocabulary is unfamiliar. Romans 3:24–5, thought by many to be pre-Pauline, speaks of Jesus as the one 'whom – God put forward as a *hilastērion*' – a Greek word whose meaning is disputed and which occurs nowhere else in Paul.[7] But do we have enough authentic Pauline material to be able to say which words were and which were not part of his vocabulary? The answer is clearly 'no'. On the whole, it seems probable that Paul himself was responsible for using this striking image. It is certainly appropriate in the context in which he uses it.[8]

Perhaps the most notable example of so-called 'pre-Pauline tradition' is to be found in Philippians 2:6–10. Once again, its 'rhythmic structure' and confessional character – the passage, like so many others, is introduced with the word 'who' – distinguish this section from its context. The use of parallelism and dramatic 'punchlines' make this a powerful summary of the gospel:

> Who, being in the form of God,
> Did not consider as something-to-be-exploited
> Equality with God,
> But made himself nothing,
> Taking the form of a slave!
>
> Having been born in human likeness,
> and being found in human appearance,
> he humbled himself,
> becoming obedient to death,
> even death on a cross!
>
> Therefore God has highly exalted him,
> and given to him the name
> that is above all names,
> that at the name of Jesus
> every knee should bow,
> in heaven and on earth and under the earth,
> and every tongue confess
> that Jesus Christ is Lord
> to the glory of God the Father!

Was this passage written by Paul himself? It is possible. It is also possible that he was making use of a 'spiritual song'[9] composed by someone else. What is clear is that – as we shall see later[10] – he uses this passage in the course of his argument in a typically 'Pauline' way.

The search for 'pre-Pauline tradition' in Paul's own letters takes us nowhere. There had probably been little time for anything but the briefest of summaries to develop before Paul's own conversion. If there *are* any quotations in his letters, they are on the whole too brief, and too close to Paul's own beliefs, to enable us to distinguish anything distinctive about his own theology. Moreover, it should be obvious that Paul would not 'borrow' any confessions of faith unless he agreed with them. What he clearly inherited, and what was certainly being preached *before* Paul, is summed up in the tradition he cites in 1 Corinthians chapter 15 – the conviction that Jesus died and had been raised from the dead – and in the confession that he had therefore been made Lord.[11]

If pre-Pauline summaries of Christian belief are difficult to discover in the letters, so too are traditions about Jesus' own teaching, of which we might have expected frequent echoes. Paradoxically, the clearest parallel between a reference to what Jesus did and said in Paul and the tradition preserved in the Synoptic Gospels occurs in 1 Corinthians 11:23–6 – the account of the Last Supper – which Paul insists he received '*from the Lord*'. Perhaps these words should be understood to mean that the tradition *originated* with the Lord, rather than as a claim to direct revelation; however, Paul is not necessarily denying that the tradition was passed on by those present at the Last Supper. Elsewhere Paul appeals to commands given by the Lord, not himself: these include the prohibition of divorce[12] and the instruction to evangelists to rely on the community for their support.[13] Other appeals to 'the Lord'[14] or 'the word of the Lord'[15] seem to reflect teaching attributed to Jesus in the Gospels, but this may have been delivered by Christian prophets speaking *in the name* of the Lord.

If we cannot deduce the pre-Pauline gospel from Paul's own writings, we may find it more helpful to compare those writings with other New Testament documents. Even though these were written subsequently they may help us to uncover Paul's unique contribution to the development of Christian thought. In what ways did Paul's understanding of the gospel differ from that of his fellow-Christians? Was he basically in agreement – or disagreement – with his fellow-Christians? And to what extent was his preaching true to the teaching of Jesus himself? Was he guilty, as has sometimes been argued, of 'distorting' the original gospel? These are questions which we cannot answer, however, until we have examined Paul's letters, and discovered what his understanding of the gospel in fact was. They are questions, therefore, to which we must return at the end of this book, when we shall be in a better position to understand and assess Paul's contribution to the development of Christianity.

2

What do we know about Paul?

Anyone wanting to write a 'life' of Paul would almost certainly turn, instinctively, to the Acts of the Apostles. Here we read, in considerable detail, the story of Paul's 'conversion' (told three times over) and subsequent missionary journeys. We learn how he endured various hazards, how he was imprisoned, shipwrecked, and finally taken to Rome as a prisoner. Luke's dramatic stories about Paul provide all the material for a classic Hollywood drama. But we are all aware of the dangers of Hollywood dramas, and their ability to distort the truth! Acts is, in effect, 'the book of the film', the presentation of a particular interpretation of Paul, *not* an attempt to discover the 'real' man behind the myth.

Luke's story

There are obvious gaps in the story that Luke tells. Paul first appears as a grown man, persecuting Christians (Acts 7:58; 8:1–3), though in the course of the story we are told that he was born in Tarsus (22:3), was a Pharisee (23:6) and had been taught by the eminent Rabbi Gamaliel (Acts 22:3), and that he was a Roman citizen (16:37; 22:25–30). We gather, too, that at some stage he had been known by the Jewish name 'Saul', rather than by the Roman name 'Paul'. But of the end of Paul's life we learn nothing: the story ends with Paul spending two years in Rome awaiting trial.

How much reliance can we place on Luke's account of Paul's middle years? A moment's thought will make us realize that we ought to hesitate before accepting even that as the framework for a reconstruction of Paul's life. Acts is the second part of a two-volume work, the continuation of the story begun in the first volume. When we turn to Part 1 – the Gospel of Luke – we have three parallel accounts with which to compare it, and it is obvious that each evangelist has told that story from his own particular viewpoint, relating incidents and sayings that are meaningful to him, and ordering the material in such a way as to bring out particular theological emphases. If Luke has done this in his Gospel, then we would expect him to do the same with Acts, and it is only the absence of the Acts of the Apostles according to Matthew, Mark and John, that makes us imagine that Luke's second book should be approached differently from his first.

As with the Gospel, Luke wrote 'Acts' with a purpose. He wanted to show how the apostles continued 'everything that Jesus did and taught' (1:1) and how they were commissioned to be his witnesses 'in Jerusalem, in all Judaea and Samaria, and to the ends of the earth' (1:8). The Eleven (together with Judas' replacement, Matthias, 1:15–26) preached the gospel in Jerusalem (Acts 2–12), while others took it to Judaea and Samaria – where their work was ratified by Peter and John (8:1–25) – and even to Phoenicia, Cyprus and Antioch (11:19). In order to show how the gospel spread 'to the ends of the earth', however, Luke needed to tell the story of Paul. Since this story ends in Rome, it is possible that Luke thought of Rome as representing 'the ends of the earth'. But if it ends in Rome because Paul's missionary work did in fact end there, with his execution, Luke perhaps intended his book as a challenge to his readers to complete the unfinished task and take the gospel *beyond* Rome, until it reached every corner of the world.

Since it was Paul, rather than the disciples of Jesus, who spread the gospel throughout the eastern Mediterranean world, Luke may have felt the need to show how Paul's work was, nevertheless, part of the Church's response to the charge given by Jesus to his eleven disciples. Certainly he says nothing about the apostles going to the ends of the earth, for he insists that they remained in Jerusalem, in spite of persecution there (8:1), and so formed the control centre of the Church. It was the Christians in Jerusalem, he tells us, who sent Barnabas to Antioch (11:22) when news reached them that Gentiles there had become Christians, and Barnabas who then enlisted Paul (still called 'Saul') to help him with this new venture. The Antioch church in turn commissioned Barnabas and Paul to take the gospel to other regions (13:1–3), and not long afterwards Luke refers to them as 'apostles' (14:4, 14), a term he elsewhere uses only of Jesus' disciples.[1] Is the term used here because Paul and Barnabas were regarded as apostles of the Antioch church? This is the solution given by most commentators, who assume that Luke has taken it over from his source.[2] If so, there is a marked difference between Paul's understanding of his status and Luke's, since Paul himself insists vigorously that he is an apostle of Christ, and that he has 'seen the Lord'.[3] Or is the word perhaps used here because Luke wants to remind us that Paul and Barnabas also had been called and sent, in the power of the Holy Spirit (13:2), just like the original group of apostles (1:8)?[4] Certainly Luke tells us that, just as the members of that group had preached the gospel and performed miracles similar to those done by Jesus himself,[5] so Paul and Barnabas now preach the gospel and perform miracles.[6] Moreover, the fact that he tells the story of Paul's conversion and call no fewer than three times demonstrates his concern to emphasize that Paul had been commissioned to take the gospel to the Gentiles by Christ himself.[7]

It was perhaps this conviction on Luke's part that Paul's missionary work was the legitimate extension of Jesus' original commission to the disciples that led him to depict Paul's travels as a series of 'missionary journeys' that brought him back to base to report. In Acts 14:24–8 Paul and Barnabas, after preaching in Cyprus, Pamphylia and Pisidia, return to Antioch and relate their success among the Gentiles to the assembled Christian community. Since

Luke tells us that the Antioch church has sent Paul and Barnabas on this journey (13:2), he naturally assumes that they will report back to the community there. When Christians from Judaea arrive in Antioch, protesting that Gentiles must be circumcised in order to be saved, Paul and Barnabas go to Jerusalem to thrash out the question there, and then return to Antioch (15:1–35).

Setting out again, Paul travels further afield and then, without explanation, sets sail for Caesarea, 'goes up' (Luke probably means to Jerusalem), greets the Church, and returns once again to Antioch, where he spends some time – though what he does there Luke fails to tell us (18:22–3). Leaving Antioch, Paul revisits his churches, and then decides to go to Jerusalem once more – this time, aiming to be there for Pentecost (20:16). He goes, not knowing what will happen there, but aware that he is heading for danger (20:22–4). Luke seems to be deliberately depicting Paul as following in the footsteps of Jesus.[8] Warned on the way that he will be 'handed over to the Gentiles' (21:11; cf. Luke 18:31–2), he declares that he is prepared to die in Jerusalem (21:13; cf. Luke 13:33). *Why* Paul thought it necessary to return to Jerusalem is not explained. When he finally arrived in Jerusalem he 'related one by one the things that God had done among the Gentiles through his ministry' (21:19). Then the Jerusalem church praised God (21:20) and approved his work (21:25).

A comparison of Paul and Acts

Our suspicions about Luke's scheme are aroused when we try to compare his account with the information provided by Paul himself in his letter to the Galatians. There he lists the visits he has made to Jerusalem since his conversion. These, of course, can only be those he had already made when the letter was written, and unfortunately we do not know when that took place – or even *the point in Luke's story* at which it might have been written. When we try to fit together Paul's account of his dealings with Jerusalem in Galatians 1 and 2 with what Luke tells us in Acts chapters 9 to 15, we find that Luke records too many visits by Paul to Jerusalem. Perhaps, then, Galatians was written *before* the meeting in Acts 15 took place; but though Luke's account and Paul's are very different, Paul's description of what he insists was only his second visit to Jerusalem since his conversion (Gal. 2:1–10) suggests that the matter under discussion was the one dealt with in Acts 15. So did Paul in fact go to Jerusalem more often than he admits? That seems unlikely, since he swears that he is telling the truth (Gal. 1:20). Perhaps, then, Luke has simply confused the various traditions he has received about Paul's visits to Jerusalem and to Antioch, and assumed that two of these accounts referred to two different visits when in fact they referred to the same one. Perhaps the importance that Luke undoubtedly attached to Jerusalem has led him to believe that Paul paid more visits to that city than he did.[9]

Luke's accounts of Paul's later visits to Judaea, too, are puzzling. He offers no explanation for Paul's visit in Acts 18:18–23, and it is possible that this is a duplicate account of an earlier visit. As for his final, fateful, visit, the first thing Paul does on arrival in Jerusalem is to visit James and report the success of his mission (21:17–20). No other explanation for his visit is given until chapter 24, verse 17, when Paul tells his opponents that he came to Jerusalem in order to bring alms to his nation and to offer sacrifices. This is the first time Luke has mentioned such a purpose, but by 'alms' he is presumably referring to the gifts that Paul collected from his churches and took to Jerusalem – and which were indeed, as we know from Paul's letters, the real purpose for his visit. These gifts, however, were for the *Christians* among his fellow-countrymen,[10] and were of enormous significance to Paul – far greater than Luke suggests.

It is Luke, then, who is responsible for the idea that Paul went on three missionary journeys, and that he returned at the end of each one, like a twentieth-century missionary on furlough, to report to headquarters and recuperate. By showing Paul as commissioned by Antioch, and as answerable to Jerusalem, he attempted to smooth over any disagreements there may have been between Paul and the Jerusalem authorities, and depicted Paul's work as an extension of that entrusted by Jesus to the eleven apostles. At the same time, however, by telling the story of Paul's conversion and call three times over, he insists that Paul had been commissioned by Christ to take the gospel to the Gentiles.

Even though Paul is clearly Luke's great hero, we can be fairly certain that Paul would *not* have approved of Luke's understanding of his activity! That he had been commissioned by Christ himself (Acts chapters 9, 22 and 26) and had been set apart by the Holy Spirit (13:2) certainly agrees with Paul's own understanding of things,[11] but his picture of Paul as having been authorized by the church in Antioch is in direct conflict with Paul's emphatic declaration that his commission as an apostle came through Christ and God the Father, and *not* through any human authority (Gal. 1:1). The Jerusalem authorities did *not* authorize him to preach, he tells us, and though, three years after he had been called by God to preach to the Gentiles, he did pay a visit to Jerusalem, he saw only Cephas (i.e. Peter, Gal. 1:18). He then preached in Syria and Cilicia – but *not* with any authority from Judaea! (1:21–2). Later, he visited Jerusalem again – not, he insists, because he needed authority, but in order to ensure that his work was not undermined by others (2:2). Although he was not answerable to the leaders of the Jerusalem church he needed their support, for it was essential that they recognized his converts as fellow-Christians. Paul tells us that the Jerusalem authorities had recognized him as an equal, and acknowledged that he 'had been entrusted with the gospel for the uncircumcised, just as Peter had been entrusted with the gospel for the circumcised: for he who was working through Peter, making him an apostle to the circumcised, worked also in me, sending me to the Gentiles' (2:7–8).

Galatians shows us clearly how Paul himself understood his commission, and it throws light also on his dispute with those who claimed to have the backing of the Jerusalem authorities. According to Acts chapter 15, certain unnamed individuals came to Antioch from Judaea demanding that gentile converts must be circumcised. Paul and Barnabas and others then went to Jerusalem to discuss the matter 'with the apostles and the elders'. In the ensuing debate, Peter is said to have reminded the company that God had chosen *him* as 'the one through whom the Gentiles would hear the message of the gospel and believe' (15:7) – a very different view from that expressed in Galatians 2:8! According to Acts chapter 15, Peter champions the position of Paul and Barnabas, affirming that 'we believe that we [Jews] will be saved through the grace of the Lord Jesus, just as [the Gentiles] will' (v. 11). Peter's words here sound like a summary of Paul's teaching in his letters, and the agreement that is said to exist between Paul and Peter corresponds with what is said in Galatians, where Paul reminds Peter of the conviction they share, that 'a person is not put right with God by the works of the law, but through faith' (Gal. 2:16). Significantly, however, the statement in Acts is attributed to Peter, not Paul! Moreover, in Galatians 2:11–21 the dispute in Antioch is said to have taken place *after* the council in Jerusalem rather than before it, as in Acts 15:1–2. In Acts, Peter is shown to be supporting Paul, while in Galatians he vacillates, and Paul has to remind Peter that salvation is by the grace of God alone. Paul, still sore from the incident, remembers that Peter failed to support him (though he *should* have done, since they shared a common belief), while Luke has clearly smoothed over the disagreement between Paul and the Jerusalem authorities.

The claim attributed to Peter in Acts 15:7 – that he is the one whom God has entrusted with the mission to the Gentiles – is significant, since it shows that Luke believes Peter and Paul to have been engaged in the same mission. Clearly Peter, based in Jerusalem, did not preach *only* to Gentiles. But neither, according to Acts, did Paul! Luke consistently shows Paul beginning his missionary work in every centre by going *first* to the synagogue and addressing Jews, before approaching Gentiles. Indeed, on three occasions, Paul despairs of winning over the Jews and declares that he will go in future to the Gentiles (Acts 13:44–9; 18:5–6; 28:23–8) – though always continuing as before. Although the problem discussed between Paul and Barnabas and 'the apostles and elders' in Jerusalem centres on the position of the Gentiles, Luke clearly does not think of Paul as preaching exclusively to Gentiles, even though in each account of his conversion this feature of his calling is mentioned (9:15; 22:15; 26:17f.). For Luke, Peter and Paul were engaged in the same mission – except that Peter remained in Jerusalem, while Paul took the gospel 'to the ends of the earth', and therefore necessarily increasingly had to proclaim it to the Gentiles.

Had Paul himself set out an account of his travels, he would clearly have told the story very differently. Did he in fact begin in each centre he came to by preaching to Jews, as Luke suggests? Tactically, an approach to the Jews would be useful, since they would naturally welcome a fellow-Jew – at least until they heard his message! But Paul believed himself to have been called to be the apostle to the Gentiles,[12] and it is inconceivable that he would preach to them only when Jews refused to listen to him. Although he would surely have seized every opportunity to preach the gospel, whether to Jews or Gentiles, he was clearly convinced that his task was to evangelize. He saw himself as engaged in a special mission, *not* part of the mission entrusted to the Jerusalem apostles, and *not* under their authority.

The 'spin' put on the interpretation of events by Luke and Paul is inevitably different. Paul's task in explaining his mission was the more difficult, for he needed to insist, on the one hand, on his independence from the Jerusalem authorities, and on the other, on his basic agreement with them – even though, on occasion, they had clearly failed to back him!

The fact that Luke tells his story in order to persuade his readers to understand events from his point of view should not surprise us: *all* historians do it! However impartial they try to be – and they do not all try very hard – they inevitably interpret events from a particular point of view. A notorious example of this is the way in which Richard III has been treated by different writers: Tudor historians depicted him as a great villain, but those of more recent times have suspected that he was being deliberately maligned by supporters of a rival dynasty. We must expect Luke's account of events – like the accounts of all historians – to be told from a particular point of view.

Luke's method of handling his material can be examined in his Gospel, as well as in Acts, and for the Gospel, we have parallel accounts from three other authors with which to compare it. But it is not easy to say how he has changed his material, since when we compare Luke with the other Gospels, we cannot be sure whether he is using them as sources, or writing independently, though drawing on the same sources that they used, or perhaps sometimes using quite different sources.[13] Since he begins his Gospel by telling us that many writers had undertaken the task of relating the events that he describes, he clearly knew several sources. The fact that he undertook to tell things *his* way, and said that he was setting them out 'systematically' (Luke 1:3), suggests that he arranged his material with a particular purpose in mind. Part of that purpose, at least, is disclosed in the way he describes the events that have taken place, since he says that these 'have been fulfilled among us'. The story he tells in his Gospel, in other words, is for him the fulfilment of God's promises and purpose, as set out in the Old Testament. In the Acts of the Apostles he deliberately continues that story (Acts 1:1). His books were not intended to be history textbooks but Christian propaganda, designed to confirm Theophilus, for whom they were written, in the faith (Luke 1:4).

Luke's sources

How reliable, then, is the information that Luke gives us about Paul? However carefully he may have collected his material,

Luke's reliability as an historian depends ultimately, not simply on the way in which he has handled that material, but on the accuracy of his sources. This, too, it is impossible to test, except by comparing what Luke tells us with information in Paul's letters – and very occasionally, in contemporary extrabiblical sources – which seems to refer to the same event.

What *were* Luke's sources in writing Acts? There are passages in the later chapters which are written in the first person plural, suggesting that one source available to him was composed by someone who accompanied Paul on some of his travels.[14] Was this perhaps 'Luke' himself? And why are so many passages *not* told in the first person plural? This suggests that the author was using traditions that had come to him secondhand. Perhaps the 'we'–passages were one source among many available to him. It has even been suggested that the use of the first person plural is merely a literary device, intended to make the narrative more vivid. Certainly it is not easy to believe that the author of Acts was himself a travelling-companion of Paul, since he shows little understanding, in what he tells us about Paul's dealings with his churches, of the issues that we know from the letters were important to him. The speeches put in Paul's mouth were probably composed, as was the custom among ancient historians, by the book's author: certainly they sometimes sound only superficially Pauline.

At times, as we have seen, Luke's account seems to conflict with Paul's, or is difficult to reconcile with it. According to Acts 17:2, for example, Paul spent three sabbaths arguing with his fellow-Jews in the synagogue, and then left the city in a great hurry, following a riot (v.14): a period of just over a fortnight is a short time to found a church which was so firmly established that it received a glowing testimonial from Paul himself in 1 Thessalonians chapters 1 to 3 – a church, moreover, which consisted of Gentile converts, who had been pagans, not God-fearers,[15] before their conversion (1 Thess. 1:9)! Luke appears to have compressed Paul's stay in Thessalonica into an impossibly short time. But other information supplied by Luke fits neatly with details given to us by Paul. Thus Paul's statement in 1 Thessalonians 3:1–2 that he stayed in Athens, waiting for Timothy to go to Thessalonica and return with news of the Christian community there, appears to tally with what Luke tells us in Acts 17:15–16.

Whom do we trust when Paul and Acts conflict? Usually, one is clearly on safer ground with Paul himself, rather than with a secondary source: Luke could easily have got the details about Paul's length of stay wrong. When Paul insists that he is telling the truth (as in Gal. 1:20), there is no reason to doubt him. But it is not always easy for one person to see 'the whole truth'. Paul tells the story from his point of view – and he, too, has an axe to grind!

Dates are obviously important for anyone attempting to write an account of Paul's life. Unfortunately it is very difficult to establish any! Acts offers a few hints, however. The most important, in chapter 18, verse 2, refers to an edict of the Emperor Claudius expelling Jews from Rome, among them Aquila and Priscilla, who arrived in Corinth shortly before Paul himself. This expulsion was dated by Orosius, a fifth-century Church historian, to AD 49: but was he accurate? Although we cannot be sure, this date seems to be supported by the reference to Gallio, proconsul of Achaia, in Acts 18:12. Fragments of an inscription found at Delphi appear to refer to Gallio as proconsul at the time of the twenty-sixth acclamation of the Emperor Claudius (whose dates are known), and this enables us to establish that Gallio was proconsul in AD 51–2.

Since there is no reason to doubt Luke's information that Paul was in Corinth 'when Gallio was proconsul of Achaia', we can reasonably assume that Paul was in Corinth in AD 51–2. Attempts to date the rest of Paul's life begin from this fixed point, but clearly depend very largely on the story as Acts tells it. Paul is described as being 'a young man' at the time of Stephen's death (Acts 7:58), but we have no firm date for that, or indeed for Jesus' crucifixion, though that may have taken place as early as AD 27. Since Paul refers to periods of 'three years' and 'fourteen years'[16] in Galatians (1:18 and 2:1) before he began his missionary work beyond Syria and Cilicia, and since he must have arrived in Corinth some considerable time after that, we can reasonably date his conversion and call to the early thirties of the first century. He was probably born at about the same time as Jesus. Since we do not know whether or not Paul died in Rome, it is impossible to date his death; but if the tradition that he was put to death there is correct, this may have taken place as early as AD 62, or perhaps in AD 64, when a persecution of Christians was unleashed by Nero.

What of the personal details about Paul provided by Acts? That he was a Pharisee (23:6) we know, since Paul tells us this himself (Phil. 3:5), but it is only Luke who tells us that he was trained by Rabbi Gamaliel in Jerusalem (Acts 22:3) and this is something that we cannot confirm.[17] It is certainly possible that he was taught by Gamaliel, since his letters reveal that he was trained in rabbinic methods of interpreting the text of scripture: there is, after all, no reason why Paul should have mentioned Gamaliel's name in writing to Gentiles, to whom it would mean nothing. But Paul usually quotes from the Septuagint – the Greek translation of the scriptures – rather than the Hebrew, and this suggests that he received his training in Tarsus rather than in Jerusalem. Was he, as Luke tells us (16:37; 23:25–30), a Roman citizen? Again, there is no reason why Paul should have mentioned this in his letters. It is sometimes argued that Paul's reference to the fact that he had been beaten with rods on three occasions (2 Cor. 11:25), a specifically Roman punishment, means that he could not have been a Roman citizen, since its use on Roman citizens was forbidden. In fact, however, there are well-documented cases where this rule was not observed. Without the necessary money or social status, Paul might well have been vulnerable. Far from home, it would have been impossible for Paul to produce the necessary documentation and witnesses to prove his claim to citizenship.

Was Paul born in Tarsus (Acts 9:11)? Paul does not tell us – but he does tell us that after his conversion he spent some time in Syria and Cilicia (Gal. 1:21). Tarsus was the capital of Cilicia, and if Paul came from that city it would be natural for him to return there. Paul's statement about his movements after his conversion also seems to confirm what Luke says. Paul went first to Arabia, he tells us, then returned to Damascus, then spent time in Syria and Cilicia (Gal. 1:17, 21). In Galatians 2:11, he is at work in Antioch (in Syria). Luke makes no reference to Arabia, but tells us that Paul left Damascus for Tarsus (9:30), and then went to Antioch to work with Barnabas (11:25–6).

It is Luke who tells us that Paul worked as a tent-maker to support himself.[18] Paul does not refer to his trade in his letters, but he does remind his readers of the way in which he had worked hard with his hands in order to support himself, rather than be a burden to others.[19] His stress on this suggests that working with his hands was not something he would normally have expected to do: in other words, he was not what we would term 'working-class'. He gave up a comfortable lifestyle for the sake of the gospel. Writing to the Philippians, he explains:

> I have learned to be content with whatever I have. I know what it is to have little, and I know what it is to have plenty. I have been initiated in all possible ways into the experiences of being full and of being hungry, of having more than enough and of going without. (Phil. 4:11–12)

Was Paul also known as Saul (Acts 13:9)? Paul never used the name in his letters, but as 'a Hebrew born of Hebrews' (Phil. 3:5), we should expect him to have a Jewish name, and 'Saul' would be appropriate for someone who belonged to the tribe of Benjamin (1 Sam. 9:15–21). It was natural for Paul to have two names, one Jewish, the other Roman.

One personal detail about Paul that Luke fails to mention is whether or not he was married. On this, Paul himself is more informative, since it is clear from 1 Corinthians 7:7–8 that he was unmarried when he wrote that letter. Moreover, he clearly believed that this brought him considerable advantages! He writes:

> I wish that everyone was as I myself am. But each person has his or her own gift from God – one this, one that. To the unmarried and to widows I say this: it is good for them to remain unmarried, as I am.

What we do not know, however, was whether he had been single all his life, or was perhaps widowed or even divorced. If he had been widowed, his reasons for remaining unattached are sufficiently explained by his arguments in 1 Corinthians 7:25–35. We should not assume that he was necessarily antagonistic to marriage.

Luke lays considerable emphasis on the fact that Paul engaged himself vigorously in the persecution of the early Christians.[20] Once again, we have confirmation of this persecution from Paul himself.[21] But what did this 'persecution' involve? Paul provides no details – simply telling us, in Galatians 1:13, that his persecution of the church had been 'excessive', and in Philippians 3:6, that it had been the result of his 'zeal'. Luke's version of the story contains improbable details. He depicts Paul (or rather 'Saul') as raiding houses and throwing men and women into prison (Acts 8:3), and as travelling to Damascus with letters from the high priest in order to bring Christians bound to Jerusalem (9:1–2). In fact, however, the high priest had no authority to make arrests in Damascus, which was in the Roman province of Syria and not in Judaea; neither, of course, did the chief priests (9:14; 26:12) or the elders (22:5). In Luke's later accounts, Paul is said to have explained how he had imprisoned and beaten believers (22:19), and had persecuted them 'to the point of death' (22:4). He had not only locked them up in prison, but had cast his vote against them when they were condemned to death (26:10). Paul is here depicted as a member of the Sanhedrin[22] – something for which we have no other evidence, and which we might have expected him to mention in his letters. Even if he were a member of that body, however, it is by no means certain that the Sanhedrin had the power under Roman rule to put people to death.[23] It looks very much as if Luke has exaggerated the effects of Paul's persecution of Christians, in order to emphasize his dramatic change of heart.

Paul himself, as we have seen, acknowledged that he had persecuted the Christians. The Greek verb (*diōkō*) that he uses to describe his activity means basically 'to pursue, seek after', and can be used in a good, as well as in a bad sense. Paul uses it again to describe his own experiences as a Christian apostle. He is being 'reviled . . . persecuted . . . slandered', he says (1 Cor. 4:12); he is 'afflicted . . . perplexed . . . persecuted . . . struck down' (2 Cor. 4:8–9) – but he continues to battle on, in spite of all these experiences. In 2 Corinthians 11:24 he is more specific: five times, he says, he has 'received from the Jews forty lashes minus one'.[24] This was the punishment inflicted in the synagogue on Jews convicted of various offences: in Paul's case, the accusation was probably laxity in keeping the Jewish regulations about food, based on the fact that he ate with Gentiles. The punishment was a common one in Paul's time, and shows that Paul was still regarded by his fellow-Jews as one of themselves, liable to the same kind of punishment that he himself had meted out to Jewish Christians in his pre-Christian days. It would seem that he had ensured that Christians who were lax in keeping the law were duly punished. Although these floggings were serious – and occasionally led to death – this is a far cry from Luke's picture of charges leading to imprisonment and the death penalty. Paul's 'persecution' of Christians would have been similar to the treatment he himself later endured; he does indeed speak of being in danger from his own people (2 Cor. 11:26), but this is probably from personal attacks and mob violence, rather than legal proceedings.

One of the most marked differences between Acts and the writings of Paul is found in their very different descriptions of his conversion – or call – though the problem here is not one of conflicting accounts, but the fact that while Luke tells the story three times over, Paul barely refers to it! This is clearly not because the event was unimportant to Paul, for he describes his 'earlier life in Judaism' (Gal. 1:13–14) and how he abandoned it for the sake of Christ (Phil. 3:4–11), and refers to himself as 'an apostle of Christ Jesus', commissioned by God.[25] Is the fact that Paul never recounts the story told by Luke in Acts chapters 9, 22 and 26 accidental? Or is it because Luke saw the value of a dramatic story, while Paul was reticent to describe his spiritual experiences (cf. 2 Cor. 12:1–10)? There can be no doubt that what happened to Paul on the Damascus road[26] was a dramatic event, but while Luke describes the blinding light and the voice from heaven, Paul speaks simply of how it pleased God to call him and to reveal his Son in and through him (Gal. 1:15–16).[27] Although we commonly describe the event as Paul's 'conversion', that term is somewhat misleading, since he was not converted from one religion to another, but rather became convinced that God had fulfilled his promises in the person of Jesus.[28] Moreover, although at this time Paul first acknowledged Jesus to be God's Son, what was of equal importance to him was his conviction that God had called him to be the one through whom his Son would be revealed to the Gentiles.

Paul's own account

With so many question-marks against Luke's account of Paul's activities, it is understandable that most historians now insist that we should begin with our primary sources – namely Paul's own letters.[29] But here, too, unfortunately, we immediately encounter difficulties.

One obvious problem is that Paul rarely provides us with detailed information about his activities. Although he might remind the recipients of his letters of what his visit to them meant for them

(1 Thess. 1:9–10) or about how he himself behaved when with them (1 Thess. 2:9–12), there was no need for him to tell the whole story of his stay among them. Sometimes, in order to avoid misunderstanding, he explains what he has done since leaving the church to which he is writing (2 Cor. 1:8–2:13), or alludes to his plans for the future (1 Cor. 16:5–9). For the most part, what Paul tells us about himself (e.g. in Phil. 3:4–6) or about his experiences (e.g. in 2 Cor. 11:22–33) or his dealings with his fellow-Christians (e.g. in Gal. 1:15–2:14) occurs incidentally, because it happens to be relevant to the point that he is making at the time. When he writes about his own calling, claiming that he is an apostle, who has 'seen the Lord' (1 Cor. 9:1), and that his apostleship is validated by the 'signs and wonders' that he has performed (2 Cor. 12:12), it is in response to those who question his authority (1 Cor. 9:2; 2 Cor. 12:11).[30] But precisely because he is writing letters, he never sets out to tell his own story, and all we have are scattered fragments of that story.

Piecing those fragments together is the more difficult because the letters are not dated: the probable order in which they were written has to be deduced from clues in the letters. Various references to the 'collection for the saints', for example, enable us to establish the order in which three of them were written: instructions for this collection are given in 1 Corinthians 16:1–4, it is clearly in progress in 2 Corinthians 8 and 9, and it is about to be delivered in Romans 15:25–9. The reference to Paul's imprisonment and imminent trial on a capital charge in Philippians 1:1–26, seems to place that letter in Rome, and so make it one of Paul's later epistles – though some scholars believe that it was in fact written from Ephesus, and that Paul was imprisoned there.[31]

Inevitably, one finds oneself turning to Acts to fill in the gaps – and there is no reason to doubt Acts' picture of Paul travelling through Syria, Cilicia and Galatia; then through Philippi, Thessalonica and Athens to Corinth: all these places are mentioned by Paul himself. Whether or not Paul's story ended in Rome, where Luke leaves him, we do not know.

But if we want to discover the real Paul, and to understand the convictions that led him, as 'apostle to the Gentiles', to set out to convert the pagan world, then we need to turn from seeking to trace Paul's life story from the dramatic account of events provided by Luke and the fragmentary information found in Paul's letters, and look at the story that Paul himself was concerned to tell – the story about how God sent his Son, born of a woman, in order that men and women might be reconciled to him.

3
A bundle of letters

If we are to understand Paul, we must turn to his letters – but when we do, we immediately confront yet another problem. There are thirteen letters in the New Testament which are attributed to Paul:[1] but did he write them all? Differences in theology, style and vocabulary make it difficult to believe that he did. So which of them did he in fact write? And how do we decide which are genuine?

Authorship

Uncertainty about which epistles were in fact written by Paul goes back to the second century, for though lists of his letters began to be compiled then, these varied in what they included. A document dating from the end of the second century, known as the 'Muratorian canon', lists nine of his letters – everything except the so-called 'Pastoral letters' (1 and 2 Timothy and Titus) and Philemon.[2] The earliest known collection of Paul's writings is found in a manuscript known as P46, written on papyrus about AD 200.[3] P46 contains most of the Pauline letters (including Hebrews!), but it, too, does not include the Pastorals or Philemon.[4] Was that because they were regarded by some in the early Church as not having been written by Paul? Or was it simply because they were not known to those who made these particular collections? When we examine the Pastoral letters, we find that the style and vocabulary of these three letters is very different from the other ten. Differences in style suggest that they were written by a different author, since literary style, rather like handwriting, tends to be distinctive. Alternatively, they could be due to use of an amanuensis – the kind of secretary who can be trusted to write a letter on one's behalf. We know that Paul used a scribe to write his letters, since he sometimes ends them in his own hand,[5] but dictating a letter is very different from saying to an assistant 'Write to so-and-so telling them such-and-such'.

The vocabulary used in any letter will depend on the matters being addressed, and differences in vocabulary can be explained if the issues that needed to be discussed at the time a particular letter was written were different from those dealt with in other letters. This is, in fact, the case with these letters. Indeed, one of the great problems with the Pastorals is that they seem to be addressed to a very different situation – and a much later one – than that reflected in the other letters. The problems that concern the author seem to be whether Timothy and Titus are faithful to the tradition which they have received, and whether those who hold office in the Church are behaving correctly. The Church seems to be structured in a way that is not reflected in other letters. Perhaps the differences are explained by the fact that the letters are addressed to individuals, and must, if genuine, have been written late in Paul's life, when ecclesiastical structures had developed. But there seem to be differences, also, in the author's approach to theological issues. Paul, as we shall discover, tends to argue from first principles, showing how the gospel implies certain modes of behaviour. The author of the Pastorals tends to appeal to tradition which must be carefully preserved,[6] and to quote credal summaries without actually drawing out their implications.[7]

Few scholars today believe that Paul wrote the Pastoral letters, though it is possible that they contain fragments of genuine letters. They provide the clearest example of the problems that face us when we ask 'Which of Paul's letters did he actually write?' Most of Paul's letters have good credentials as we have seen: they were included in early lists of his writings and in early manuscript collections of his letters. The questions to be asked concern internal evidence, and depend very much on comparisons between the letters. For this, we need to establish a 'norm' – a letter which everyone will agree is authentic. Here, Galatians is the obvious starting-point, since it is written with such passion and indignation that only Paul himself could have been responsible! Romans is in many ways very similar to Galatians, both in style and vocabulary. 1 and 2 Corinthians and Philippians deal with rather different issues, but seem to be recognizably Pauline in style and vocabulary, as does 1 Thessalonians. The brief letter to Philemon is universally accepted as authentic. After that, agreement ceases! Scholars differ as to whether Paul wrote 2 Thessalonians, Colossians and Ephesians, and though their conclusions are based on scholarly arguments about the use of vocabulary, stylistic differences, and differences or developments in theology, there is a strong subjective element in any decision.

Some years ago, two scholars set out to apply what they considered to be 'objective' stylistic tests to the Pauline letters.[8] They concluded that Paul himself wrote only five of the letters attributed to him: Romans, 1 and 2 Corinthians and Galatians – together with Philemon which, though too short to be submitted to stylistic analysis, could be included because there was no reason to exclude it. To explain the other letters, they postulated several different authors, arguing that stylistic evidence suggested that Ephesians, Philippians, Colossians, 1 and 2 Thessalonians and 1 and 2 Timothy had come from five different hands! Their attempts to provide 'objective' analysis were unsuccessful, however, for even if the literary tests they used were reliable (which was disputed) there are too many problems with trying to analyse these texts in this way.[9]

Fortunately, as we have seen, there is general agreement that Paul wrote seven of the letters that bear his name. Decisions about which of the other letters he actually wrote will inevitably reflect individual scholars' presuppositions, and the way they interpret Paul's thought. Can we, for example, envisage the Paul of Philippians developing the kind of Christology expressed in

Colossians? Could the situation addressed in Ephesians – so different from that reflected in Galatians – have existed already in Paul's day? Since our only knowledge of his later theology and the situations he addressed is deduced from the letters themselves, the answers we give to these questions can only be tentative. If we want to discover Paul's own thought, therefore, it is best to begin with those letters about which we may be reasonably confident – Romans, 1 and 2 Corinthians, Galatians, Philippians, 1 Thessalonians and Philemon – and to use the others – 2 Thessalonians, Colossians and Ephesians – with caution, remembering that they may tell us more about the way in which Paul's teaching was developed by his followers than about Paul himself.

In our modern world, we are likely to feel that there is something morally wrong in attributing one's own work to someone else, and we regard documents which claim to have been written by someone more famous than the actual author as fakes. We have all heard of forged diaries, which attempt to influence people's perception of history, or of paintings passed off as the work of great artists. These things are clearly done in an attempt to deceive – usually for financial gain. If some of the letters attributed to Paul were written by others, however, it is likely to have been for a more worthy motive. Christians who revered Paul and had been taught by him may well have written these letters after his death, because they believed that they were interpreting his message for a later generation. As time passed, situations changed and new problems arose: the growth of the Church, for example, meant that rules regarding church discipline needed to be established – the kind of rules that we find in the Pastorals. What would Paul have said in these changed circumstances? Whoever wrote these letters probably sincerely believed that they were preserving and passing on the Pauline tradition. The fact that they attempted to apply his teaching to their own situation by writing letters in his name shows how important Paul was to those who had come under his influence.

What the authors of these 'deutero-Pauline' letters were attempting to do – reinterpret Paul's teaching for their own day – has been done again and again down the centuries by commentators who expounded Paul's teaching in the light of their own culture and society. Christian teachers such as Augustine, Luther, Calvin and Wesley, for example, all applied Paul's teaching to problems and concerns of their own day. For them, of course, Paul's letters were authoritative because they were regarded as 'scripture'. Their reinterpretation made Paul's writings relevant to their own day – but would probably have puzzled Paul's original readers!

Fragmented information

Our search for the 'real' Paul is essentially a search for his beliefs. Paul was the first theologian of the Christian Church, and he has a good claim to be regarded as its greatest, for he understood the implications of the Christian message in a way that became formative for those who came after him. At this point, however, we encounter yet another problem in our attempt to understand Paul. Theologians normally write books – frequently very long ones, published in multiple volumes – but all we have from Paul is a bundle of letters. Now letters are clearly 'occasional' literature, intended to address a particular situation, and often written at great speed in order to 'catch the post' – which, in Paul's case, meant entrusting the letter to someone who was travelling (either as his personal envoy, or else on business) to a particular city. Letters are not meant to be theological treatises![10] Paul's letters contain personal greetings and news, and deal with particular issues of concern to the community. He deals, for example, with questions as varied as 'Does a Christian man need to be circumcised?' 'Should Christians eat meat that has previously been offered in sacrifice to pagan gods?' 'What will happen to Christians who have died?'

'How should Christians behave?' In his replies to these questions, Paul invariably refers to the theological principles which provide the basis of the Christian life, which means that we find theological gems – succinct statements of belief – scattered throughout the epistles. But these scattered statements are a very long way from the carefully ordered tomes of later theologians, setting out a systematic account of their doctrine of God, creation, Christ, redemption, the Holy Spirit, the Church, and the end of all things.

Attempting to reconstruct Paul's theological beliefs by reading his letters is rather like attempting to improve one's school French by reading a French novel without the aid of grammars or dictionaries. Even though details of the story will be misunderstood, being plunged into the way that the language is used will help one to understand its principles, and should prove far more interesting than poring over the grammar books.

Paul was essentially a practical and pastoral theologian. Even in Romans, the nearest thing to a treatise among his letters, he did not set out to write a 'systematic' theology, but to deal with particular issues that were troubling his churches. He was constantly thinking on his feet, working out the implications of his faith and discovering new ways of expressing it. This makes reading Paul more exciting and more challenging than reading any 'straightforward' book of theology. For what we see in his letters is Paul *applying* the Christian gospel to every situation. Are the Thessalonians worried about the future? There is no need, since 'our Lord Jesus Christ . . . died for us, so that whether we are awake or asleep we may live with him' (1 Thess. 5:9–10). Are the Corinthians succumbing to gluttony and immorality? 'You were bought with a price; therefore glorify God in your body' (1 Cor. 6:20). Does Paul wish to encourage his churches to contribute to a weekly collection (1 Cor. 16:1–3)? He urges them to remember 'the grace of our Lord Jesus Christ who, though he was rich, yet for your sakes became poor, so that by his poverty you might be made rich' (2 Cor. 8:9). Have some of them misunderstood his teaching about the resurrection? Then he must remind them of the good news which he proclaimed to them (1 Cor. 15:1–11). These brief summaries of the gospel help us to understand not only *what* Paul believed, but how he thought that belief to be relevant to everyday life and practice.

Piecing together a 'theology' of Paul is thus a kind of detective-story. We need to gather those scattered gems and string them together. But alas, we shall find that some important ones are missing, and that the resultant necklace will be imperfect. And one of our problems is that we do not know what is missing! We do not know what Paul *might* have said, had the problems that arose in his churches been somewhat different. Think, for example, of what is included by chance. It is only because some of the Corinthians were apparently in danger of turning the celebration of the Lord's Supper into an occasion for over-indulgence that we have Paul's account of the institution of this rite (1 Cor. 11:23–6), an account earlier than those provided by Matthew, Mark and Luke. It is only because some of the Corinthians had problems with the belief in future resurrection that we have Paul's summary of the tradition that had been passed on to him concerning Christ's death and resurrection, and of his appearances to his followers (1 Cor. 15:1–7). It is only because Paul, facing the prospect of imminent death, wanted to remind the Philippians that the story of Christ's self-sacrificial love which he preached was also the model for his own ministry and must be the model for their way of life, that we have the important christological 'hymn' in Philippians 2:6–11. How much more we might have known about Paul if we had more of these letters! Paul's theology is like an iceberg: we see *some* of it in his letters, and are impressed by what we see, but we know that there is far more to it than is actually visible to us.

The information conveyed in letters will inevitably be patchy, since the issues discussed will tend to be those that have given rise to misunderstanding or dispute. Paul often has to take his congregations to task because they have not grasped particular implications of the gospel. What they have understood correctly does not need to be discussed. There is a certain resemblance, therefore, between what Paul says in his letters and the answers given by a lecturer to the questions posed *after* a lecture: sometimes these questions ask for further amplification, sometimes they display total or partial misunderstanding of what has been said. Important points that have been fully understood or which are common assumptions held by both lecturer and audience will not need to be repeated.

We have Paul's answers to the questions – but we rarely have the questions themselves. Yet another problem we have to face is that one person's letters give us only *half* the picture. We do not know what was said in the letters addressed *to* Paul, or by those who brought him news of what was happening in his churches, and we therefore have to reconstruct the situation as best we may. The dangers of misunderstanding this situation are obvious to anyone who has overheard one end of a telephone conversation and leapt to the wrong conclusion!

We need to heed one more warning before we turn to reading Paul's letters. It is difficult – perhaps impossible – for us to put ourselves into the shoes of someone from another time and culture. As L. P. Hartley famously expressed it: 'The past is a foreign country: they do things differently there.'[11] All of us read documents in terms of our own understanding of the world and of society. In the case of Paul, the differences between his world and ours are enormous. In addition to the obvious differences between the ancient world and our own, there were differences in social and cultural values, many of which are far from obvious. Even when we may think we are on safe ground, because Paul is using terms – such as 'the Son of God' – that are familiar because they are central in later Christian teaching, we need to remember that in Paul's own day, their meaning may have been rather different, and certainly did not include the doctrinal implications given to them later.

We have to remember, too, that Paul had been born and brought up as a Jew, and that the gospel he proclaimed concerned the surprising way in which the God in whom he had always believed and continued to believe had fulfilled his promises to his people. The Christian community, even though it was now – largely through Paul's own activity – expanding into the gentile world, had not yet broken away from its Jewish roots. Arguments which Paul had with his fellow-Jews about the place of Gentiles within the Christian community seemed of little relevance to later generations of Christians who were now all Gentiles. As time passed, Jews were regarded as enemies, and Paul's letters came to be read through anti-Semitic spectacles, which badly distorted their meaning. As we shall see, this misunderstanding not only gave rise to further hatred between Jews and Christians, but did a grave injustice to Paul. We need to attempt to understand why he wrote as he did if we are to avoid such tragic misunderstanding.

4

Paul's inheritance

Paul had been born and brought up as a devout Jew. Listing his Jewish privileges in his letter to the Philippians, he tells us that he had been 'circumcised on the eighth day' (i.e. according to the requirement of the law), and that he was 'a member of the people of Israel, of the tribe of Benjamin, a Hebrew born of Hebrews'; in regard to the observance of the law, he was a Pharisee (Phil. 3:5–6).

As a Jew, Paul believed that there was one God (Deut. 6:4), whose name, YHWH (usually translated 'the LORD' in our English Bibles) had been revealed to Moses at the burning bush (Exod. 3:14–15). This God was the creator of the whole universe (Isa. 40:12–31; 45:18), but had chosen the Israelites to be his special people, and had brought them out of Egypt. He had revealed himself to Moses on Sinai, and had entered into a covenant with the Israelites there (Exod. 19:3–6). On his side, God had promised to care for Israel as his treasured nation, while on theirs, the people had promised to obey his commands, set out in the law. After disciplining the people in the wilderness, God had settled them in the Promised Land, where he continued to speak to his people through the prophets. This God was clearly a loving God, who had shown his nature by caring for his people and saving them from their enemies. He was also a righteous God, as the commandments given on Mount Sinai made plain.

Because Jews have always understood their God to be a God who acts, their beliefs about him were expressed in the form of narratives. The story of Israel came to be seen as part of an even bigger story, which began at the beginning of time, when YHWH created the world, and everything he made had been good. But because men and women had disobeyed God, he had punished them. Their sin had led to strife among themselves, to struggle with the forces of nature, and to the worship of false gods, but God had called Abraham to follow him, and had made a covenant with him, promising him that he would bless his descendants. It was through the descendants of Abraham – i.e. the people of Israel – that he planned to fulfil his purpose for the world.

Throughout their history, God had guided and guarded his people, but they had been rebellious and had sinned (Jer. 2:7). Since God was in control of his world, the fact that Israel had been overrun by her enemies and the people taken into exile was interpreted as divine punishment (Isa. 30:1–5; 8–14), but God could use foreign rulers to restore her good fortune, as well as to destroy it (Isa. 45:1–7). He had forgiven his people and brought them back from exile, showing himself to be a God of mercy. And since, in spite of Israel's failings, God remained faithful to his covenant promises, he would ensure that those promises were finally fulfilled: those Jews who had kept faith and obeyed the law would be rewarded, and Israel would be restored to peace and prosperity under the rule of a descendant of David (Isa. 11:1–9).

The end of this story still lies in the future, but it will arrive only when God once again establishes his rule on earth. When rebellion is finally crushed, and all creation is obedient to God, then Paradise will be restored. The change envisaged by the biblical writers was so dramatic that it could be described as the creation of a new heaven and a new earth. Meanwhile, the task of the pious Jew was to obey God's commands faithfully. For those who died before the End, there was a hope shared by some Jews – including the Pharisees – of resurrection (Dan. 12:2).

But the End would bring punishment as well as reward. For those who had been disobedient, and who had defied God's commands, the final day of reckoning – the Day of the Lord – would be a day of judgement and wrath (Joel 2:2). God's punishment would be poured out on the wicked in Israel, as well as on the Gentiles.

The fulfilment of the promise

When Paul was confronted by the risen Christ on the Damascus Road he did not cease to be a Jew, or abandon his Jewish beliefs. He was not converted *from* Judaism; rather, he was converted to the belief that Jesus was the promised Messiah, and so the fulfilment of all his Jewish hopes.

We have to understand, then, that Paul's new faith took shape within the context of the beliefs in which he had been brought up. He continued to believe in the God of his forefathers, and shared the Jewish abhorrence of idol-worship. When taking the gospel to Gentiles, he would often have to persuade them to 'turn to God from idols' and 'to serve a living and true God' (1 Thess. 1:9). It was only within the context of this belief in the one true, living God, that a message about how he had sent his Son made sense. But though there is only one God, there *are* 'so-called gods' (1 Cor. 8:4–5), and pagans who sacrifice to idols are in fact sacrificing to demons (1 Cor. 10:19–20). Like other Jews, Paul believed that there were dangerous powers seeking to control men and women (Rom. 8:38–9), and refers several times also to the hostile activity of Satan.[1]

Acceptance of what is called the 'eschatological framework' of history – the belief that God had created the world and would fulfil his purposes by bringing his creation to a perfect fulfilment – also remained an essential element in Paul's understanding. God had created the world (Rom. 1:20, 25), but men and women had sinned (Rom. 5:12); condemnation and punishment had followed, and worse would follow on the day of judgement (Rom. 2:1–11), but now the process has been reversed in Christ (Rom. 5:15–21). With the resurrection of Christ, we have what is in effect a new creation and the dawning of the new age (2 Cor. 5:17).

For Paul, the covenant that God made with Abraham continued to be important – but now he understood this covenant to have been fulfilled in Christ (Rom. 4:1–25; Gal. 3:6–18, 29).

He continued to believe, too, that God had revealed himself to Moses (2 Cor. 3:7–18), and that the law that had been given to Israel through Moses was holy, just and good (Rom. 7:12); but he believed that God had revealed himself more fully and acted more decisively in his Son (2 Cor. 3:10; 4:4; Rom. 8:3). God had spoken, also, in the past through the prophets – but now their words were understood to point forward to Christ.

Paul the Christian is still 'an Israelite, a descendant of Abraham, a member of the tribe of Benjamin' (Rom. 11:1), and he acknowledges the role that Israel has played as God's chosen nation. God has worked through his people, by 'adopting' them and revealing his glory to them. He gave them the covenants, the law, the privilege of worshipping him, and his promises for the future. The patriarchs, too, 'belong' to Israel, and from Israel, by human descent, Christ himself was born (Rom. 9:4–5). Throughout history, God has worked through Israel, and he has not abandoned his chosen nation now (Rom. 11:2).

Paul insists that God stands by his promises (Rom. 9:6). God's promises to Abraham *have* been fulfilled – through Christ. He has *not* rejected his people (Rom. 11:1). He *has* revealed his purpose and his will in the words of the law and the prophets – which is why Paul constantly appeals to them. Scripture is for Paul the authoritative 'given' on which he bases his arguments. Its ethical demands shape his assumptions about what is and what is not appropriate behaviour.[2] Law and prophets between them influence his understanding of how best one could love God and love one's neighbour.

Paul's education

Paul's description of himself in Philippians 3:5–6 suggests that he had been brought up as the child of devout Jews. From his childhood, he would have been taught to read the scriptures, and would have known much of them by heart. In particular, he must have studied what Jews referred to as 'Torah',[3] the first five books of what we now call the Old Testament.[4] As a Pharisee, Paul would have devoted himself to the study of the Torah, and would have been concerned to observe every detail of the Mosaic law set out there; he would have been familiar also with the oral traditions discussing its meaning and setting out how it could be obeyed. His eagerness in these matters is summed up in Galatians 1:14, where he writes: 'I advanced in Judaism beyond many among my people of the same age, for I was far more zealous for the traditions of my ancestors.'

Paul's familiarity with Jewish methods of exegesis is seen again and again in his letters. What his gentile readers would have made of his arguments one wonders, for he seems to assume that his audience possessed an intimate knowledge of the scriptures and an ability to follow the kind of reasoning that would have been used by the rabbis. Would his readers have had the skill and knowledge to follow his arguments? This way of handling the scriptures is particularly prominent in Galatians and Romans, probably because both are concerned with the question of how Gentiles can become members of the people of God, and with the special role of Israel. The arguments Paul employs in these two letters probably reflect the debates he had with those Jewish Christians who saw the matter differently from himself. The skills he had learned as a Pharisee were now being used for a new purpose.

It is clear from his writings, however, that Paul had also been given a Greek education, and it was this education that enabled him to communicate with the many different peoples of the eastern Roman Empire, where the *lingua franca* was Greek. Significantly, when Paul quoted from scripture, he almost always seems to have used the Septuagint, the Greek translation that was widely used by Jews of the Diaspora. Although he describes himself as 'a Hebrew born of Hebrews' (Phil. 3:5) – almost certainly meaning that he spoke Hebrew at home – he was familiar with the scriptures in translation.

The Greek education that Paul would have received in Tarsus (assuming the tradition recorded by Luke to be correct) would have been based on reading Homer and other great classical authors, and would have been concerned with learning the rules of rhetoric. Children were themselves taught how to write by studying the writings of others, and learning the rules that governed the composition of speeches and letters. With the advent of e-mail, conventions regarding letter-writing rapidly broke down, but we are still aware of what are considered to be the appropriate ways to begin and end formal letters. In the ancient world, conventions about how to compose a letter or a speech were carefully studied and practised, so that following them probably became instinctive. Analysis of Paul's letters has shown that they, too, generally follow the expected pattern for a letter written at that time. But because Paul's letters were intended to do more than simply convey greetings or news, and were normally sent in order to persuade the recipients about a particular point of belief or behaviour, they sometimes seem to follow the pattern that we would expect to find in a speech.[5]

Paul appears to have felt more at ease when writing than when speaking. Certainly there seem to have been times when his letters made more impact on others than did his speeches. Writing to the Corinthians – who, since they lived in a city which prized culture, may well have set great store by the rhetorical skill of their leaders – he shows that he is aware that some of them concede that 'his letters are weighty and strong', but consider 'his speech contemptible' (2 Cor. 10:10). His Greek is forceful, not elegant.

Was Paul influenced in other ways by Greek culture? That he was aware of it there can be no doubt, for it was all about him. In every city there were magnificent temples to the gods. Paul was certainly conscious of them – even though, as a Jew, he mocked the worship that took place there (Rom. 1:23), and denied that idols had any real existence (1 Cor. 8:4–6). In the lecture-halls, philosophers debated their theories. Paul undoubtedly knew this, and may well have been aware of their arguments – though once again, he regarded their quest for wisdom as vain (1 Cor. 1:18–25). Occasionally Paul seems to refer to sayings or beliefs of well-known philosophers: in 1 Corinthians 15:33 he apparently quotes Menander when he writes 'Bad company ruins good character', though the saying may well have been proverbial; the view expressed in 2 Corinthians 4:18, contrasting 'what is seen' with 'what is not seen', sounds superficially like Plato,[6] while that in Philippians 4:11 – 'I have learned to be content (or self-sufficient) whatever my circumstances' – is close to the Stoic view, although similarities do not necessarily imply borrowings.

In the early twentieth century, it was often argued that Paul was influenced by the mystery religions, which were popular in the ancient world. These religions – which were many and various – offered their devotees the power and protection of a particular god in this life and hereafter. Contrary to popular belief, however, there is no evidence to suggest that the initiate was identified with the dying-and-rising deity – the idea that is central to Paul's understanding of Christian baptism. Moreover, the cults seem to have promised rebirth rather than resurrection. Paul's converts may well have seen analogies, but he is unlikely to have derived his beliefs from the mysteries.

The imperial cult would have been very familiar to Paul. The emperor was hailed by his subjects as 'Lord' and 'Saviour', and even as 'Son of God' – all titles that Paul used of Christ. Once again, Paul did not derive these titles from Rome, for they came into Christian usage from the Old Testament, but such terms would have rung bells in the minds of his converts. The Christian gospel was inevitably seen as a challenge to the imperial cult. For Christians, as for Jews, Caesar was not divine, and the titles he claimed belonged by right to another.

As well as receiving the instruction that any Jewish child would have been given, and a Greek education that equipped him as a powerful writer, Paul was familiar with the culture and society of his day. The extent to which he was a debtor to these three influences on his life has been much debated. Certainly his writings would have presented challenges to the assumptions and mores of the Roman Empire. His Greek education made him a skilled communicator. But it was his Jewish faith that had shaped his beliefs and attitudes, and which continued to influence him. Far more important than all of these, however, was Paul's encounter with the risen Christ, which made him rethink many of his old assumptions. His new experience inevitably created tensions with the traditions he had inherited from the past. What resulted from these tensions we must consider next.

5

The new element

What was the new element in Paul's understanding of the world, the experience that transformed his Jewish beliefs? In 1 Corinthians 15:1ff., he reminds the Corinthians of the tradition that he had himself received, and had in turn passed on to them: it concerned the death and resurrection of Christ. In summing up this tradition, Paul uses four verbs: Christ died and was buried; he was raised and appeared – to a long string of witnesses, including, finally, Paul himself. The two key events here are Christ's death and resurrection: just as the burial confirmed the reality of his death, so the appearances confirmed the reality of his resurrection.

We have here the kernel of the gospel – of the good news[1] – that Paul had preached to the Corinthians. This good news concerned the death as well as the resurrection of Christ, since the resurrection was not understood as simply the reversal of a mistake: the death of Jesus was explained as having taken place 'for our sins', and both death and resurrection were said to be 'according to the scriptures'. In other words, both were part of God's plan, and were seen as the fulfilment of his purposes, which had been set out in the Jewish scriptures. What was new was the conviction that God had once again acted, this time in the person of Jesus, who was his Messiah, or anointed one, and who had been confirmed as his agent by the resurrection.

The resurrection

For Paul, this conviction stemmed from his encounter with the Risen Christ, who had called Paul, the persecutor of Christians, to be an apostle (1 Cor. 15:8–11). Paul describes his call as a kind of premature birth, which may seem a strange expression to use, since he was, he tells us, the *last* of those to whom Christ appeared. Yet this metaphor reminds us of the abrupt nature of his conversion/call. There had been for him no preparatory 'gestation' period as a disciple of Jesus: instead, he was suddenly confronted by the Risen Christ.

1 Corinthians 15 has little to say about the death of Christ, and a great deal to say about his resurrection. That is because Paul's concern, in this chapter, is to deal with a misunderstanding of his teaching to the effect that there is no future resurrection for Christians. This idea Paul dismisses as absurd. He spells out the evidence for Christ's resurrection here because he believes that the future resurrection of believers depends on that of Christ and will be like his. Christ has already been raised – a fact to which many witnesses testify – and his resurrection is, says Paul, like the 'first fruits' of the crop, a guarantee of more to come (v. 20). Why? Because of Christ's status as 'the last Adam'. What Christ did, and what happened to him, affect the fate of others in a way similar to that in which what Adam did and what happened to him affected all humanity. If Christ has already been raised, then those who belong to him will be raised in the future.

Paul is working here within the eschatological framework which he had inherited from Judaism, and already he has used two names for Jesus which come from Judaism – 'Christ', and '[the last] Adam'.[2] At the beginning, Adam had sinned and been punished by death: his descendants had shared in his fall.[3] Jewish hope for the End included God's sending of the Messiah, the resurrection of the faithful people of God, and life in a renewed paradise. With the resurrection of Christ, Paul believes, the End has in a sense begun, even though the old order of things seems to be continuing as before. The resurrection of Christ means that final restoration is in sight, and God's purposes for his creation will soon be achieved. Paul expects Christ to return and to destroy every hostile authority and power (v. 24). His coming will be the signal for the resurrection of those who belong to him (v. 23). When everything is restored, Christ will hand over the rule to God himself (v. 28).

Paul's understanding of the future is essentially Jewish, with one additional feature – his conviction that Christ has already been raised from the dead. Since resurrection was part of the Jewish expectation about what would happen in what was termed 'the age to come', in contrast to 'the present age', this meant that the age to come had in a sense already begun. The future has broken into the present. What that signified for Christians here and now, Paul spells out elsewhere.

As we have seen, Jewish ideas about the End included the expectation that God would restore everything in the universe to conform to his original intention for creation. The death and resurrection of Christ meant the beginning of this restoration process: just as Christ had died and been raised, so those who joined themselves to him had in a sense already died to the old world and been raised into a new one. Through Christ, men and women had been brought into a right relationship with God, and had begun to live in obedience to him. The mark of this new life was the power of God's Holy Spirit working in their lives (Rom. 5:15; 8:1–2).

We can represent the overlapping of the ages in the following way:

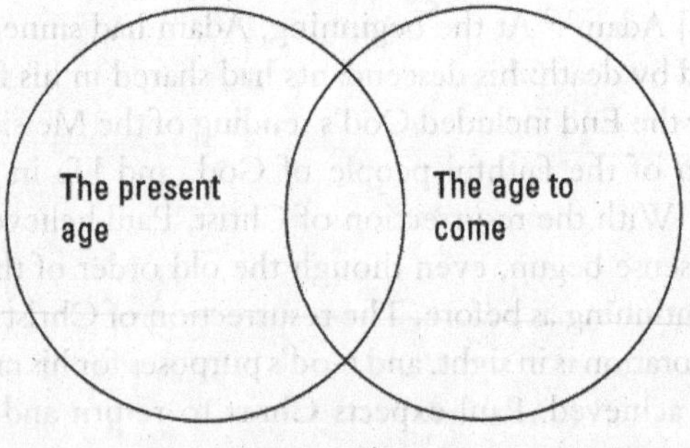

The conviction that the End has in a sense arrived is sometimes referred to as 'Realized Eschatology'.[4] It is perhaps better to use the term 'Inaugurated Eschatology', however, for though the End-time has begun, it has not finally arrived.[5] Believers are, in effect, living simultaneously in two ages, still subject to the limitations of the present age, but already experiencing the gifts that belong to the age to come. In 1 Corinthians 15, Paul is concerned to remind the Corinthians of what still lies in the future.

Although God is the chief actor in 1 Corinthians 15 – it is he who raises Christ from the dead (v. 15) and who will raise Christians (v. 52) – it is Christ who is at the centre of the action, the one *through* whom God works. If it was Paul's experience of the resurrection – his encounter with the Risen Christ – that transformed his understanding of God's purposes, this was because it was this experience that convinced him that the crucified Jesus was indeed 'Christ', the Messiah. That recognition brought with it the acknowledgement that the crucifixion itself had been part of God's saving purpose – an idea which he had previously regarded as blasphemous.

A scandalous message

With the conviction that Jesus was God's Messiah, and that he had been raised from the dead, therefore, came also the transformation of Paul's understanding of his death. In 1 Corinthians 15, he tells us simply that Christ died 'for our sins', and 'in accordance with the scriptures'. He does not tell us what that phrase 'for our sins' means, nor does he explain which scriptures he has in mind. Earlier in the letter, however, he has reminded the Corinthians that the one thing he had preached to them had been 'Jesus Christ, and him crucified' (2:2). It is clear from 1 Corinthians 15 that Paul does *not* mean that he did not preach the resurrection to them! The message of *Christ* crucified made no sense without the resurrection. But it is also clear that to the pre-Christian Paul this message had been worse than senseless. As he puts it in 1 Corinthians 1:23: 'We proclaim Christ crucified, a scandal to Jews and foolishness to Greeks.' The early Christians did not proclaim this message out of choice! The crucifixion had taken place, and it needed to be explained. In seeking to explain it, they found its significance.

In the modern world, it is difficult to appreciate the absurdity – the apparent impossibility – of this 'good news' about 'Christ crucified'. Two millennia of Christian interpretation have anaesthetized us to the horrors of crucifixion, and turned the cross into a symbol of glory. The reality was anything but glorious. Crucifixion was a common form of execution in the ancient world, favoured by the Roman authorities because it inflicted the maximum pain and humiliation on those they were punishing. The victim was nailed up naked, and left to die a lingering and horribly painful death. Paul's contemporary, the Jewish historian Josephus, described it as 'the most wretched of deaths'.[6] The Romans used it primarily to punish disobedient slaves and those members of subject nations who rebelled against Rome.

One can understand, then, why Paul recognized that his message appeared to be sheer folly. The cross was a symbol of weakness and degradation: what kind of a god allowed his chosen representative to be put to death in this hideous and shameful way? It is hardly surprising, too, that he refers to it as 'a scandal'. But the fact that he speaks of it as 'a scandal to Jews and folly to Greeks' is more than mere rhetoric, for the Christian gospel must have seemed particularly scandalous to Jews.

To discover why, we need to turn to Galatians, a letter which begins more abruptly than any of Paul's other letters, and which reminds the Galatians straight away of the essential fact that God had raised Jesus Christ from the dead (1:1). Then, once again, we find Paul referring to the belief that Christ had died 'for our sins', and explaining that this had set his followers free 'from this present evil age (1:4). In chapter 3 he reminds the Galatians of the gospel he had preached to them: he had, he says, 'placarded the crucified Jesus Christ' before their eyes (3:1). And because they had believed his crazy message that God was at work even here, they had experienced the power of his life-giving Spirit. Verses 10–14 of this chapter explain why this message is a 'scandal' to Jews. According to the law, criminals who were condemned to death and who were hung on a tree were under the curse of God, and so became a curse to the land (Deut. 21:22–3). How, then, could God have allowed his chosen anointed one to have been crucified, branded by the law as an offence to God himself, and a source of infection to others? We can imagine Paul *before* his conversion, indignantly rejecting Christian claims for Jesus and quoting Deuteronomy 21. Paul knew precisely why the gospel he now preached was 'a scandal to Jews'. But he had discovered that Christ's death had the opposite effect to the one described in the law: it had brought, not a curse, but blessing. Only belief in the resurrection could make sense of this experience and this message.

Without the law

The letter to the Galatians gives us some insight also into why Paul's conversion – his conviction that God had indeed raised Jesus from the dead, and that he was indeed the Messiah – was so inextricably bound up in his mind with his commission to be the apostle to the Gentiles. Jesus had suffered a death which branded him as a lawbreaker, and an offence to God. Yet God himself had vindicated him, raising him from the dead and so recognizing him as righteous. There could be no clearer demonstration of the fact that righteousness before God – that is, being in a right relationship with God – does not depend on obedience to the law. On what, then, *did* righteousness depend? Two very different factors pointed Paul to an answer.

First, as a Pharisee trained in the interpretation of sacred writings, he turned to scripture. Tracing back God's covenant with his people to Abraham, he observed that God's promises had not depended on Abraham's obedience to God's law, which had not yet been revealed. 'Abraham believed God,' he read, 'and this was reckoned to him as righteousness' (Gen. 15:6). In other words, acceptance by God depended simply on the grace of God and trust in his promises. If righteousness before God did not depend on observance of the law, then Gentiles, as well as Jews, could be included among God's righteous people. This is the basis of Paul's argument in Galatians 3:6–9.

Secondly, Paul was confronted by what was happening in the Christian community. In Galatians 3:1–5 he asks the Galatians to consider their own experience: they had believed the gospel message and received the Holy Spirit. In other words, they were experiencing the joys of 'the age to come' and living in a new relationship with the risen Christ without ever having converted to Judaism. God was clearly not confining his grace to those who observed the law, but was pouring it out on Gentiles. They were being treated by God himself as though they were members of his people Israel.

The Galatians' experience was, of course, the *result* of Paul's missionary work. But had something similar occurred earlier, which had persuaded Paul himself that Gentiles had been included in God's people? Interestingly, we find the same argument being used in Acts 10:1–11:18, though there it is attributed to Peter. In Acts 10, Peter preaches to a group of Gentiles – Cornelius and his household – who receive the Holy Spirit and are baptized. The evidence that persuades Peter (and subsequently the Jerusalem church) that Gentiles are to be recognized as full members of the new community is the fact that they have already received the Holy Spirit. It is therefore clearly unnecessary for Gentiles to observe the law in order to be members of the new community (Acts 10:9–16).

Can we rely on Luke's account of this incident? Could he even have been influenced in telling this story by what he had learned from Paul himself? That is possible. But there is evidence in Paul's own testimony that some of those who were Christians before him – and so enjoying the experience of living in 'the Age to come' – were less than scrupulous in their observance of the law. If there is one thing that is certain about Paul's early life, it is that before his conversion he had persecuted the Christian community (1 Cor. 15:9; Gal. 1:13; Phil. 3:6). As we have already seen, this suggests that Christian Jews were being found guilty of failing to keep the law. But *why* should this happen, unless it was because they were mixing with Gentiles, who had responded to the gospel? Was this what caused Paul's fury, and his savage treatment of the Christians? If so, his conversion inevitably meant the acknowledgement that God's salvation had already been at work *outside* the law (Rom 3:21); Jews who had been lax in observing the law (and possibly Gentiles too) were in a right relationship with God while he, Paul, zealous in keeping the law, had – because of that very zeal – unwittingly opposed God's Messiah! He was bound to conclude that the great turning-point in history had not taken place, as he had always believed, on Mount Sinai, but on Golgotha, the site of Jesus' crucifixion. From now on, what distinguished those who belonged to God's people was not whether or not they kept the law, but whether or not they had faith in what God had done for them in Christ.

But who and what was this person whom Paul refers to repeatedly as 'Christ', and why had God chosen to act through him? It is to this question that we turn next.

6

Who was this Jesus?

One of the extraordinary features of Paul's writings is that he uses the word 'Christ' almost as though it were a proper name. As a Jew, Paul knew very well that the word was *not* a proper name, and that it was the Greek translation of 'Messiah', the Hebrew word meaning 'anointed'. The term was used in Jewish writings to refer to someone appointed by God to fulfil a particular task: sometimes it was applied to Israel's king,[1] and so also (though not in the Old Testament itself) to the *expected* Davidic king,[2] but it was also used of others who were chosen and used by God.[3] The character and function of the Messiah were by no means as clearly defined as later Christian re-interpretation of the Jewish texts has led people to believe, but one thing is clear: the 'Messiah' was selected by God to play a particular role in his plans for his chosen people Israel.

Messiah

It is often suggested that the way in which Paul uses the word 'Christ' shows that it had very quickly taken on the character of a name, and that its original meaning had been forgotten. Strangely, Paul uses the word as a title rather than as a name only once – in Romans 9:5. Gentiles, it is argued, would not have understood the significance of the word. Perhaps not, but it is Paul who is writing and he certainly understood its significance! For the first Christians, who were all Jews, the term would have been full of meaning. It was the starting-point of Christian understanding of Jesus' identity, as the Gospels all suggest,[4] even though, on its own, it proved inadequate to express all that was believed about him.

The fact that Paul uses the word so often suggests that for him, the belief that Jesus was God's Messiah was essential. As Messiah, Jesus was God's agent in the world, and the fulfilment of all God's past promises to his people, and his death and resurrection were 'according to the scriptures'. His messiahship was essential to the divine plan to restore the peace and prosperity of Israel.

But why, we may wonder, did Paul, who saw himself as called to preach to *Gentiles*, insist that *they* should acknowledge Jesus as Christ? Why did he not simply proclaim Jesus as 'Lord' or as 'Son of God' – two titles that he uses, though far less often, and which would have had far more meaning for Gentiles than the term 'Christ'? The answer to these questions lies in the continuity between God's saving activity in the past and in the present. The gospel proclaimed by Paul was new, but it was not a new religion. The God who had called Israel to be his people was using Israel to fulfil his purposes. The Davidic king had been seen as the representative of his people, and his legitimate descendant had the same role. Paul acknowledged Jesus to have been 'born of the seed of David according to the flesh' (Rom. 1:3) and to be the Messiah of Israel 'according to the flesh' (Rom. 9:5). He was thus the legitimate representative of his people.

But now, with the resurrection of Christ, the whole scene had been transformed, because the definition of 'God's people' had been changed. The descendants of Abraham – who was regarded as the father of Israel – were discovered to be those who shared Abraham's faith – that is, faith in the God who gives life to the dead (Rom. 4:17, 24);[5] in other words, Abraham's true descendants are not the Jews, who claim him as their ancestor 'according to the flesh' (Rom. 4:1), but all those, whether Jews or Gentiles, who believe that God raised Jesus from the dead. The identity of the people of God has been redefined, and no longer depends on human ('fleshly') credentials. God's promises to his people have been fulfilled – but have been found to be far more inclusive than had been imagined.

How had this happened? Through the death and resurrection of Christ which, as we have already seen, inaugurated the new age. Because he had been raised, the age to come was already here. Christ's resurrection, then, was not simply a guarantee of future resurrection, but the source of new life here and now. Paul describes this new way of life as 'life according to the Spirit' in contrast to 'life according to the flesh', the life which belongs to the present age. We should not be misled into thinking that he regarded flesh as evil: it was simply weak. In Jewish thought, 'flesh' represented weakness, while 'spirit' represented strength: 'flesh' stands for human frailty, over against 'spirit', which is the power of God (Isa. 31:3). Life in the present age continued, but the resurrection of Christ had inaugurated the new age, and with it the possibility of living 'according to the Spirit'.

We can now represent life in the two ages as follows:

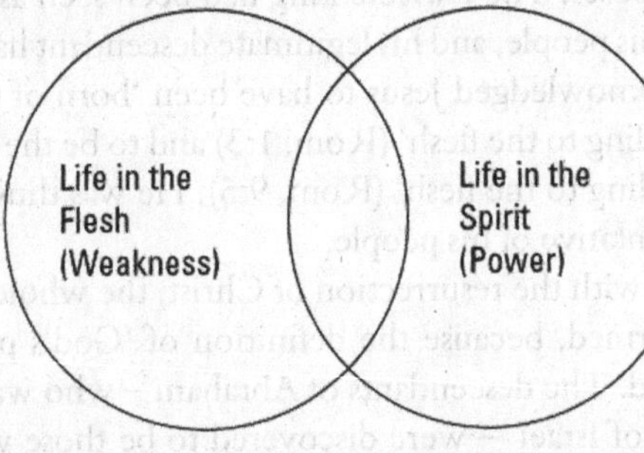

Christ himself had been born and died in the old age – the age of the flesh – but he had been raised into the new. Until the End finally arrived, however, the weaknesses and suffering associated with *this* age would inevitably continue.

We might perhaps think, then, that Paul's references to Jesus being the Jewish Messiah 'according to the flesh' are simply dismissive: if that were all that could be said about him, he would have been Israel's Messiah, and nothing more. However, the 'new creation' that comes with Christ's resurrection (2 Cor. 5:17) is not a beginning from scratch, but a *re*creation; not a creation *ex nihilo* ('from nothing'), but a redemption, a continuation and completion of the old story. It is the same God who is at work in the present as in the past, and he has not forgotten his promises to his people. For Paul, it is essential that Christ himself was born into 'the old age', in order to redeem it and transform it. It is *because* he was Israel's Messiah 'according to the flesh' that he is also able to be 'Christ' for the new people of God in the new age. We shall discover, as we explore Paul's letters, that this idea that Christ shared our humanity is vitally important.

In the opening verses of Romans, Paul remarks that the gospel brings salvation 'first to the Jew, then to the Greek'. That principle is fundamental, for God revealed himself to the Jews in the past, and promised to complete his purpose for the world through them. Later in the epistle he likens Israel to an olive tree that has had branches broken off and into which wild olive shoots have been grafted. This strange horticultural procedure demonstrates Israel's central role in God's plan. The past had *not* been abandoned. We can understand, then, why Paul almost invariably referred to Jesus as 'Christ', rather than simply as 'Jesus': it was a way of expressing one essential aspect of his identity. The term 'Christ' reminds us of the essential continuity between past and present, between what God had been doing in the past and what he was doing now. It is not really either a title or a name, but rather a word that refers to the role played by Jesus as the representative of his people. What that involves we shall see later.

Both names and titles are summary statements, a means of conveying, in shorthand, qualities and functions that could be spelt out in a long description of what someone is and does. The words 'the King', for example (provided we know the time when and the place where the king is functioning), tell us a great deal about an individual's ancestry, his powers and his duties. But the confession that 'Jesus is the Messiah', meaningful in a Jewish context, would have conveyed little to Gentiles in the ancient world. Had

Paul arrived in a town and proclaimed this message in the marketplace, his hearers might well have retorted, 'Who is what?' To convey the significance of his message Paul needed other terms. Once again these came from Judaism and had been used by Jewish Christians before Paul, but unlike 'Messiah', these other terms would have been meaningful in the pagan world.

Lord

First, we note that Paul frequently uses the title 'Lord'. Several times in his letters he refers to the confession 'Jesus is Lord'.[6] The substance of the message he proclaimed was, he says, 'Jesus Christ as Lord' (2 Cor. 4:5). The belief that this confession goes back to the Jewish community is supported by Paul's use of the Aramaic word *marana,* 'our Lord', in 1 Corinthians 16:22. In the Jewish world, it was an appropriate term for anyone in authority – for example the king (Ps. 110:1) – though it could also be used as a respectful term of address (e.g. Gen. 19:2).

The Greek word for 'lord', *kurios,* had also been used to translate the Hebrew name of God, YHWH, which was too sacred to be pronounced. Paul, who quotes often from the Septuagint, was certainly aware of this special meaning. Yet he refers to Christ consistently as 'Lord'. Remarkably, there are even occasions when Old Testament passages referring to God appear to be taken over and reapplied to Christ.[7] But Paul is clearly not simply identifying Jesus with God, since it was God who raised Jesus from the dead, proclaiming him as 'Son of God' and 'Lord' (Rom. 1:3–4; 10:9). Those who call on the name of the Lord will be saved because of what *God* has done (Rom. 10:13, 9). In 1 Corinthians 8:6, Paul quotes from the *Shema'* – the summary of belief about God in Deuteronomy 6:4–6 which is recited daily by Jews – but adapts it by distinguishing between the one God (the Father) and the one Lord (Jesus Christ). Jesus exercises some of the functions of God,[8] but even though he is acknowledged to be the 'one Lord', he himself is obedient to the authority of his Father, who will finally be acknowledged as 'all in all' (1 Cor. 8:6; 15:27–8). For Paul, the term 'Lord' is an appropriate term for the one who, under God, exercises authority in the world and is worthy of all honour. Indeed, Christ's proclamation as 'Lord' is a means of honouring God (Phil. 2:11).[9]

In the pagan world, *kurios* could be used of both rulers and gods (cf. 1 Cor. 8:5). In the Roman Empire, Emperors came to claim divine honours, and as a result there was a growing emphasis on the imperial cult. Though Paul himself did not challenge the claims made by the state in his day (Rom. 13:1–7), he would certainly have refused to acknowledge Caesar as *kurios* had that been demanded of him. By the end of the first century AD, the confessions that 'Jesus is Lord' and 'Caesar is Lord' were recognized as expressing conflicting loyalties, and the proclamation of Christ as Lord was seen as subversive.

Son of God

Paul's use of the phrase 'the Son of God' or 'God's Son' is less common than the terms 'Christ' or 'Lord', but is important nevertheless. Writing to the Romans, Paul announces that the gospel is 'about God's Son' (Rom. 1:3). It is worth asking what the statement that a person is someone's son would imply in secular life. It conveys, first of all, the idea of legitimacy, and so of the *privileges* that belong to someone who is acknowledged to be his father's son. Secondly, we expect a certain similarity between father and son. The son is not necessarily the spitting image of his father, but we expect a degree of likeness in looks, gestures and character. Thirdly, in the ancient world if not today, it was assumed that a son had certain duties towards his father – primarily, the duty of *obedience*. These three aspects are relevant in trying to understand what might be meant by the statement that Jesus is 'the Son of God'.

Once again, the phrase has a background in Judaism. In the Old Testament, we find that angels were sometimes referred to as 'the sons of God' (Gen. 6:2; Job 1:6). Israel is also referred to as God's son – an appropriate image, since it reminds us, on the one hand, of the privileges given to God's chosen nation, and on the other, of the obedience expected from a child to its father. The term is an apt one for the people who are in a covenant relationship with their God (Exod. 4:22; Hos. 11:1). God is called the Father of Israel (Deut. 32:6; Jer. 3:19), and the people of Israel are his children (Deut. 14:1; Isa. 43:6). Israel proved to be a disobedient son, however, and was often chastised as a result. Some individuals were obedient, and later traditions, such as that found in the book of Wisdom, spoke of the righteous man as 'the son of God' (Wisd. 2:18).[10]

The king, representative of the nation, is sometimes referred to as God's son (Ps. 2:7; 89:26–7). 2 Samuel 7:14, referring to David's son Solomon, is particularly interesting, since it came to be interpreted of the future king.[11] Clearly, the term was an appropriate one to use for the Davidic Messiah.[12] But, like the term 'Messiah' itself, the phrase 'the Son of God' was broader in its meaning than this 'royal' use. The term 'son' in these various contexts is a statement about a relationship rather than a title.

In the Hellenistic world, there were many stories about children of the gods – sometimes gods themselves, sometimes outstanding men, such as Apollonius of Tyana, a contemporary of Jesus, who was credited with miracles.[13] The Stoics regarded Zeus as the father of all (cf. Acts 17:28). Kings in the Ancient Near East were accorded divine honours and regarded as sons of the god, and the title was taken over by Rome and given to the Emperor, although it does not seem to have been used *as a title* for anyone other than the Emperor. Nevertheless, to those living in the Hellenistic world, 'Son of God' would have appeared to be a comprehensible name for Jesus in a way that the foreign term 'Christ' would not.

What did the phrase 'the Son of God' mean for Paul? Since he uses the term seldom, it is worth looking at what he tells us about God's Son, in the hope that we may be able to answer this question. No fewer than half of the occurrences of the term are found in Romans.

As we have noted already, he tells the Romans that his gospel is 'about God's Son' (Rom. 1:3, 9). Clearly the belief that Jesus is God's Son belongs to the central core of the gospel. But while spelling out the content of that gospel, Paul uses the term once more, explaining that the gospel is 'about God's Son, who was descended from David according to the flesh', and who was also 'declared to be Son of God by the resurrection' (Rom. 1:4). In other words, the resurrection was God's way of vindicating Jesus, declaring him to be righteous, and acknowledging him to be his Son.

Moving on to Romans 5:10, we find another succinct statement of the gospel: 'If, while we were enemies, we were reconciled to God through the death of his Son, how much more, being reconciled, shall we be saved by his life.' Our reconciliation to God is achieved by the death of his Son, and we therefore have nothing to fear. Why did Paul use the term 'Son' in this context? Is its appearance here accidental? Would his statement have had the same meaning if he had chosen to refer to 'Christ'? Since Paul does in fact use 'Christ' in the parallel statement in v. 8, the answer to that question may well be 'Yes'. Nevertheless, the use of the phrase 'his Son' here does serve to emphasize the unity of purpose between God and Christ. The loving purpose of God is achieved through the obedience of his Son Jesus, and the death of Christ is the result, not of God's displeasure, but of the Son's obedience to his Father's will. Reconciliation between God and human beings has been brought about, not by the action of God alone, but by an action in which Father and Son were at one. Moreover, since reconciliation was the purpose of both Father and Son, and was achieved in this costly way, we can be confident that God's love will continue into the future, and that we shall be saved from future wrath. As Paul said in Romans 1:3, the gospel *is about God's Son*. His use of the title 'the Son of God' in Rom. 5:10 underlines his confidence in the loving activity of God, which has been demonstrated in the past through his Son, and so can be guaranteed to continue in the future.

The remaining references to 'the Son of God' in Romans all occur in chapter 8. In verse 3 we find another famous summary of the gospel: 'What the law could not do . . . God [has done], sending his own Son in the likeness of sin and flesh.' Paul's theme is once again the loving purpose of God, which has been achieved through sending *his Son*. The law was unable to do what it promised, because of the weakness of the flesh and human disobedience, but God has now achieved his purpose by working through the obedience of his Son. What was that purpose? Not simply to condemn sin and fulfil the law's command (vv. 3–4) but to conform men and women to the likeness of his Son, who is the firstborn among many brothers (v. 29).[14] Paul has already spelt out how this happens in verses 9–17: Christians live in the Spirit, not the flesh, because they have received the Spirit of God (v. 9), and those who have received that Spirit are in fact God's children (v. 14), and call him 'Abba',[15] which means 'Father'. Paul's use of the term 'God's Son' here serves to remind us, not only that he sent Jesus to fulfil his purpose, but that this purpose was in fact to create in men and women a similar obedience: the Son's relationship to God is a model for theirs.

In this chapter, Paul sets out his conviction about God's plan for the future. God's purpose is to restore the whole creation to what he intended for it (vv. 19–39). Paul is confident that this will eventually happen, and that God's purpose for restoration is secure because of what he has already done for us. Paul's logic is exactly parallel to that which underlines his argument in Romans 5:8–11. Since God 'did not spare his own Son, but gave him up for us all,' we can be confident that 'with him, he will give us all things' – i.e., everything else that God has promised us (v. 32).

The one who has given up his Son for us will not abandon his plans! Our future is thus guaranteed.

The argument of Romans is in many ways similar to the one Paul used in his earlier letter to the Galatians. Unusually there, however, in Galatians 1:15, Paul refers to his conversion/call. He describes it in this way: God 'was pleased . . . to reveal his Son in me, so that I might proclaim him among the Gentiles'. Here too, therefore, as in Romans, Paul begins his argument from the reminder that the gospel is *about God's Son*. Because what we know as Paul's experience on the Damascus road is normally thought of as a conversion, rather than as a call, Paul's account of what it pleased God to do is normally translated as 'to reveal his Son *to* me'. Translators assume that Paul is referring to his vision of the Risen Christ. But the Greek preposition *en*, which is used here, means primarily 'in' or 'by', rather than 'to', and perhaps that is what he meant! If so, then, it would seem that he is thinking, not simply of what God revealed *to* him, but of what God was to reveal *in* him – both by means of the message that he was to preach to the Gentiles and, just as important, through his manner of life as a Christian. In other words, God chose to reveal his Son to the Gentiles, not only in the gospel Paul proclaimed but also in what he himself became at his conversion – an adopted son of God, whose way of life was being conformed, through the work of the Holy Spirit, to become like the Son of God himself (Rom. 8:15, 9, 29). What Paul understood by 'the gospel of God' was not simply something to be proclaimed, but something to be lived. The message of that gospel – love for others, and life through death – is, as it were, stamped upon him.

It is hardly surprising, then, to find Paul spelling out what this means at the end of the next chapter. He has, in effect, he tells us, been crucified with Christ (Gal. 2:19). But Christ was raised from the dead, and now lives – and lives, Paul claims, in him; the result is that it is no longer really he, Paul, who lives, but Christ who lives in him (v. 20). We understand now what Paul means by being 'conformed to Christ's image'. His life as a Christian is controlled by the Son of God, who loved him and gave himself up for him (v. 20). Paul used here the verb he was to use later in Romans 8:32, but in Galatians he speaks of the Son of God giving *himself* up, rather than of God giving up his Son. The use once again of the term 'the Son of God', however, is perhaps intended to remind us that what happened was God's purpose, and that it was willingly carried out by one who knew his will.

Finally in Galatians, we find Paul describing how 'God sent his Son, born of woman, born under the Law' (Gal. 4:4). His purpose was both 'to redeem those under the Law', and also so that 'we might become sons of God' (v. 5). That this has happened is authenticated by the fact that God has now sent the Spirit of his Son into believers' hearts, and that they cry 'Abba, Father'. What Paul said here is very close indeed to what he says later in Romans 8 – and once again, as there, we have the problem of 'sexist' language. To Paul, of course, living as he did in a patriarchal society, this was not a problem. Indeed, it is as well to remember that the problem of sexist language did not arise until the last quarter of the twentieth century! Until then, 'masculine' language was (unless the context made the opposite clear) understood to include the feminine, and it was only the rise of the feminist movement that highlighted this as a symbol of female exclusion. When Paul referred to Christians here as 'sons', he certainly did not intend to exclude women, since in the previous paragraph he insisted that in the new community that exists 'in Christ', there is no division between male and female (Gal. 3:28).

Many translators attempt to avoid this problem by using the word 'children' instead of 'sons', but this leads to two further difficulties. The first is that this translation destroys the link between Jesus as Son and Christians as sons, so that it is really necessary to refer to him by the less specific – and so less personal – term 'the Child of God'. The second is that, by using the word 'sons', Paul is deliberately affirming the *privileges* that belong to God's people. In the ancient world, privilege belonged to sons, and not to daughters. In Galatians 4, he is contrasting the privileged status of sons over against slaves, but in the previous chapter he has discussed this in terms of inheritance, and it was *sons* who were entitled to inherit their fathers' property. In Galatians 3:28, he insists that in the new era that has been inaugurated by Christ all who believe are 'the offspring of Abraham' – i.e., members of God's people – whether Jew or Gentile, slave or free-born, male or female. Women have an equal share in this inheritance! And that means that, in Christ, they all have the status of 'sons of God' (Gal. 3:26).

In the twenty-first century, Paul's language appears unacceptably sexist. We need to remember, however, that in the ancient world, Paul's description of all Christians as 'sons of God', far from being 'sexist', was the very opposite! His use of this term was an affirmation that all Christians – both men *and* women – were full members of the new community, and that none of them were second-class citizens.

In Galatians and Romans, Paul's use of the term 'the Son of God' reminds us that God himself is behind what takes place in the life, death and resurrection of Jesus, and that Jesus himself willingly accepts this vocation. It reminds us, also, that there is an important link between what the Son of God is and what men and women are intended to become, living in a loving and obedient relationship with God their Father.

Paul uses the term in a similar way in his other letters. In 1 Corinthians 1:9 and Colossians 1:13, for example, it occurs in opening 'reminders' of the gospel which his readers have accepted.[16] 1 Corinthians 1:9 declares that 'God is faithful' – and the fact that he has called the Corinthians 'into the fellowship of his Son' is perhaps intended to underline that faithfulness. In 2 Corinthians 1:19, Paul's own reliability is founded on God's faithfulness, and that faithfulness is demonstrated by the fact that the Son of God himself, on whom Paul relies, is God's 'Yes' to all his promises, the fulfilment of all his plans. In 1 Thessalonians 1:10 we find

Paul using 'the Son of God' in yet another reference to the gospel which his readers received. Paul reminds the Thessalonians here that they believe that God raised his Son from the dead; this being so, they can rely on him to save them from future wrath. The argument is once again the one he employed in Romans 5:8–11: if God has done this already, through his Son, we can rely on him for future salvation also. The Age to Come was inaugurated in the death and resurrection of God's Son, and Christians can be sure that he will keep them safe when it finally arrives. Finally, we should take note of 1 Corinthians 15:28, which speaks about the End of all things, when the Son himself will hand over rule to God and be subject to him: his mission is accomplished when God's rule over the world is restored.

Paul's use of the term 'Son of God' for Jesus reminds us of something very important about Paul's theology, which is that even though his letters are of necessity 'Christocentric' – since the *new* element in Paul's understanding of God had come through the life, death and resurrection of Jesus – his theology remains theocentric, since it is about what God has done '*through* Christ' (2 Cor. 5:19; cf. Rom. 8:3).

This perhaps explains why Paul tells us so little about Jesus *apart* from his theological statements about him. To be sure, he tells us that Jesus 'was born of a woman, under the law' – in other words, that he was Jewish – but this is a theological, rather than a biographical statement, emphasizing the oneness of the Son of God with humanity and with fellow Jews. So, too, as we have seen, is Paul's statement that Jesus was of Davidic descent (Rom. 1:3; 9:5). Of Jesus' life Paul tells us nothing, apart from noting his 'obedience' (Rom. 5:19), which may, indeed, refer rather to his death (cf. Phil. 2:8). And though there may be echoes of Jesus' teaching in several of the letters, there is no clear quotation of his words, and no account of any of his actions. Paul focuses instead on the death of God's Son, who was handed over by God (Rom. 8:32) and raised by the power of his Father (Rom. 1:4; 6:4; 1 Cor. 15:12–20).

We have looked in some detail at the way in which Paul uses this particular title because there is no clearer example of the way in which later doctrines and presuppositions can distort our understanding of an ancient text. Paul wrote long before the fathers of the Church had got to work trying to formulate their beliefs about Christ. The questions they asked were often very different from the questions that occurred to Paul, and their answers tended to be expressed in philosophical language quite foreign to Paul's. For them, too, Christ's sonship meant oneness with the Father, but it was oneness of essence rather than oneness of will. For Paul, *who* the Son is was expressed in what he did. As Son, he is like God, and so his actions – including his self-humiliation and willingness to accept death – show us what God himself is like. The Son of God is the one who, because he was obedient, carried out God's will. As God's Son, Christ was sent by God to fulfil God's purpose – which was, as we have seen, to enable men and women to become his children.[17] Later theologians seized on such statements and asked questions about what the Son was doing *before* he was sent, so opening up a debate about Jesus' pre-existence. In order for Christ to have been sent, they argued, he must presumably have been already present with God. Paul's concern in these statements, however, is not with pre-existence, but with the fact that Christ alone was able to carry out God's purpose, because he alone was totally at one with his will.[18] The idea of 'sending' implies that God was behind all that the Son did. Like the prophets before him, he was sent, and was obedient to God's will (Jer. 7:25; Luke 11:49); but because he was the Son of God, he did more than proclaim the prophetic word and perform the prophetic action, since he revealed the nature of God himself. Wisdom, too, was said to have been 'sent' by God, in order to reveal the ways of God to men and women (Wisd. 9:10), as Jesus does now.

By his obedience, the Son had fulfilled the law's requirement (Rom. 8:4) to love God with heart and soul, mind and strength, and to love one's neighbour as oneself.[19] How Christ and Torah (law) are related we must consider next. That topic, too, will tell us more about who Paul believed Jesus to be, for the question 'Who was he?' cannot be answered simply by looking at his names and titles.

7

Christ: the 'end' of the law

Central to the Torah, the teaching given by God to his people, was the law revealed to Moses on Mount Sinai. On Sinai, the people of Israel had agreed to obey the commandments set out in this law, as their part in the covenant between God and themselves. The law was the bond between God and Israel, the sign that they were his people, and so a prized possession.

It is clear that Paul's attitude to this law is inextricably linked with his own experience. In Philippians 3, he sets out his privileges as a Jew: he was 'circumcised on the eighth day, belonged to the people of Israel, was a member of the tribe of Benjamin, a Hebrew born of Hebrews; as far as keeping the law was concerned, a Pharisee; as far as zeal was concerned, a persecutor of the church; regarding the righteousness specified by the law, blameless' (Phil. 3:5–6).

Paul is well aware of the value of the privileges that he had once prided himself as possessing: value, that is, in terms of 'the flesh' (Phil. 3:4), for these assets belong to the *present* age, the age of the flesh, and Paul has exchanged them for something far more precious. Like the man in the parable who sells everything he has in order to buy the one pearl of surpassing value (Matt. 13:45–6), he has given up all these things in order to gain Christ, and to be found 'in him' (Phil. 3:7–11). Using the image of a profit-and-loss ledger, Paul says that he has 'written off' all these assets, treating them as garbage. His conversion meant a total reappraisal of what he valued.

Gentiles and the law

Paul's description of his Jewish privileges as 'garbage' (Phil. 3:8)[1] seems highly derogatory, and would surely have offended his fellow-Jews. But Paul is writing here to gentile Christians, not to Jews. We need to remember that his purpose in this passage is to underline the contrast between the privileges he enjoyed as a Jew and what he now possesses as a Christian, in order to put the Philippians on their guard against those who might try to persuade them that, as *Gentiles,* they were still outsiders, and needed to accept circumcision and undertake to obey the regulations set out in the Jewish law in order to be acceptable to God. The Jewish Christians who argued in this way,[2] and who insisted that it was only by becoming Jews that Christians could belong to God's people, are dismissed by Paul as 'dogs'. The term is one that Jews used of Gentiles, and Paul's use of it here means that he is in effect saying that those who rely on their Jewishness 'according to the flesh', rather than on what God has done through Christ, are *themselves* the 'outsiders'; these people, he says, do evil (though they pride themselves on their righteousness) and *mutilate* the flesh by insisting on circumcision. In contrast to what he has now discovered to be of supreme value, Paul regards his Jewish privileges as worthless. To insist that others need these things in order to belong to God he considers to be positively harmful.

Paul's conversion, as we have seen, was linked in his mind with his call to be the apostle to the Gentiles. In Galatians 1:13–16, he again refers to the zeal that had characterized his 'earlier life in Judaism'. But then had come an event which he describes as taking place at the time 'when God was pleased . . . to reveal his Son through me, in order that I might proclaim him among the Gentiles'. The result of Paul's conversion had not been a mere chance development: it had been the *purpose* of God's revelation to him – a revelation which had taken place in order that Paul might proclaim his Son to the Gentiles; it was for this that God had set Paul apart before he was born, and it was for this purpose that he was called by God's grace. Paul's attitude to the law had been profoundly changed, not simply by the fact that he had now found something far more precious than the law, but also by his conviction that the gospel entrusted to him was intended for Gentiles *as* Gentiles – that is, for those *outside* the law.

As the apostle to the Gentiles, Paul had founded gentile Christian congregations, and his letters were written to gentile Christians. Scholars differ in their assessment of the make-up of the Pauline churches: it would be absurd to suggest that there were no Jewish members in these communities. There were Jews resident in many of the cities to which Paul travelled, and some of these will certainly have responded positively to the message proclaimed by Paul and by others. But he deals primarily with gentile converts,[3] and his stand on the law is governed by this fact.

We have seen how Paul's starting-point – both as Christian and as apostle – is Christ's resurrection. It was his conviction that Christ had been raised from the dead that made him a Christian, while it was his vision of the Risen Lord that qualified him to be an apostle (1 Cor. 9:1). We have also seen that for Paul this meant that the age to come had already arrived. Paul's attitude to eschatology[4] is of vital importance for understanding his position regarding the Gentiles.

Paul was by no means the first Jew to insist that God was not the God of Jews alone (Rom. 3:29–30; 10:12). Indeed, the fundamental Jewish affirmation that God was the only true God meant that he *must* be the God of all nations. The belief that God had entered into a special relationship with his people Israel was held side by side with the conviction that he was the creator of the world and the lord of history.[5] Part of the prophetic expectation for the future age was that the Davidic king would be established, not simply as the ruler of Israel, but as the leader of the nations (Isa. 55:3–5). Israel is understood as having been called to be 'a light to the Gentiles' and 'a covenant to the people'

(Isa. 42:6). Undoubtedly this was sometimes understood to mean that other nations would acknowledge Israel's God, and so recognize the superiority of *Israel* (Isa. 60:1–16; 62:2), but the idea that Israel is to be a light to the nations is also understood to mean that God's salvation will be extended to 'the end of the earth' (Isa. 49:6; 51:4–5): the Gentiles themselves are included in God's plans for a restored world. God will establish his teaching throughout the whole earth (42:4), and people will flock to Jerusalem to worship the Lord and learn his ways (2:2–4). Nations will join themselves to the Lord and become his people (Zech. 2:11; 8:20–3).

Since Paul believed that the Last Days expected by the prophets had arrived with Christ's resurrection, he saw the conversion of the Gentiles as the fulfilment of the prophetic promise (Rom. 9:25–6). But what did that imply? Some Christians argued that Gentiles should therefore obey the teaching set out in the law given to Israel: that was surely only logical. Just as Gentiles wishing to convert to Judaism had been expected to become proselytes, and to observe all the requirements of the Jewish law, so now Gentiles who believed that the promises had been fulfilled in Christ needed to take on all the privileges and obligations of the Torah. There was certainly no reason for Jews to *abandon* the teaching given to them on Sinai, and every reason why Gentiles who now acknowledged Israel's God should accept it. For Gentiles who had responded to the gospel, the next step forward must therefore be to become Jews. It is clear that some Jewish Christians were advocating this view among Paul's Galatian converts.

But there was an alternative view, which was based on the Jewish belief that when the last days came there would be no further *need* for the law, because everyone would obey God: the law would, in effect, be written on their hearts (Jer. 31:31–4). Paul's insistence that the Gentiles do not have to put themselves under the law is entirely consistent with this: the Spirit of God would guide them and show them what they should do. Proof that he was right to maintain this was, he believed, plain, since his gentile converts had *already* received the Spirit (Gal. 3:1–5), one of the signs of the 'last days'.[6] Having received the Spirit, there was no need for Gentiles to put themselves 'under the law'. Far from being a step *forward,* that would be a step *back.*

So what should the Jew who became a Christian do? The regulations set out by Moses concerning worship and daily life were, for Jews, the obvious way for them to express their devotion to God, and continued to be so. There was no reason why the Christian convert should abandon the practices of the law (1 Cor. 7:17–20); no reason, that is, unless obedience to the law actually *conflicted* with the new life in the Spirit enjoyed by those who belonged to Christ. And this is precisely what happened in Christian communities where there were both Jews and Gentiles.

The problem arose when Jewish and gentile Christians began to eat together. It was clearly the custom in the early Church to meet together for a meal, as a symbol of their fellowship in the new community (Acts 2:46),[7] but Jews were expected to follow strict rules regarding the preparation of food, and this caused obvious problems when Jews and Gentiles started sharing meals. Were the Jews to insist that the food must all be prepared in accordance with the law – so imposing its regulations on Gentiles – or were they to abandon its rules, and eat whatever they were offered? Certain Jewish Christians insisted that these joint meals should not take place (Gal. 2:11–13). Paul protests, because he sees the experience of freedom in Christ being challenged by the food regulations. The old requirements (which he regarded as belonging to the old era of the flesh) were undermining the unity of the community that belonged to the new era of the Spirit, and they must not be allowed to destroy it. When the problem arose in Antioch, Peter himself had, in Paul's view, been misled, since he had stopped eating with gentile Christians (Gal. 2:12). But as Paul reminded Peter at the time, his behaviour was inconsistent since he, like Paul, knew that the way to be brought into a right relationship with God was *not* by obedience to the law, but by faith in what God has done through Christ (Gal. 2:15–16).

What is true for Gentiles, then, proves to be true for Jews also. Since God is God of both Jews *and* Gentiles, he restores both of them to a right relationship with himself in exactly the same way – by faith, and *not* by the 'works' set out in the law (Rom. 3:27–31). If the same Lord is Lord of all, this must mean that there is no distinction between Jew and Greek, and that he works in the same way to save them both (Rom. 10:12). Paul was now convinced that this way was through Jesus Christ, crucified and risen, and *not* through the works of the law.

This new understanding of how God was at work left Paul with a problem, however. As a Jew, he continued to believe that God had chosen his people, Israel, and had revealed himself to Moses at Sinai. The law God had revealed to Moses was, Paul insisted, holy, and its commandments were just and good (Rom. 7:12). Yet Israel had failed to observe those commandments (Rom. 2:23–4; 3:10–20); the people whom God had saved and made his own had proved disobedient (Rom. 10:21). The problem was that the law itself had seemed to promise life to those who obeyed its commands.[8] But the law was operating in what Paul terms the sphere of the flesh, which is characterized by weakness, and where sin is an invasive and deadly force. The result was that men and women were unable to obey the law (Rom. 7:7–13), and so the law was unable to give them the life that it promised (Rom. 8:3). The law had proved ineffectual in preventing sin; Christians, however, have been 'discharged from the law' (Rom. 7:4–6), since God had now done, in Christ, what the law had been unable to do (Rom. 8:3–4).

The law's true purpose

It might seem as though the law had a design-fault built into it, but though Paul's argument seems, at times, to imply this, he never draws this conclusion. Indeed, he could not, for the law had been given by God! If there is a fault, it is not in God himself or in his *purpose*. If the law has been unable to give what it appeared to promise, that is the fault of sin which, as we have seen, exploited the weakness of the flesh. But since God is God, he must have known that this would happen. Perhaps, then, the problem was that Israel misunderstood the true *purpose* of the law.

In Galatians 3, Paul explains that the law had been an interim measure, a temporary expedient introduced in the period between the time when God had first made his promises to Abraham and the moment when he fulfilled them in Christ (Gal. 3:15–18). But why was it introduced? In order, Paul says, to keep sin in check (3:19–25). We might well ask: but why was this interim period necessary? Paul does not deal with this question, and he does not need to, because the problem he was addressing was a more urgent one, namely the situation that existed in the Galatian churches, where Galatian Christians were being told that the law was necessary for their salvation. Far from being necessary, retorted Paul, it was – as a system of rules – out of date, belonging to a bygone age. Life under the law belongs to the age of weakness, the age of the flesh, 'the present evil age' (Gal. 1:4) from which the Galatians have been set free.

Paul begins his argument in Galatians 3 by appealing to the Galatians' own experience. Since they had received the Spirit when they responded to the gospel, it should be plain to them that their new relationship with God has come about through faith, not by obedience to the regulations set out in the law (3:1–5). But this principle, says Paul, is set out in the law itself, which states that Abraham, the father of the Jewish nation, had been 'reckoned as righteous' because he had believed God. As a result, God had promised to bless all the nations through Abraham (3:6–8). The promises given to Abraham were prior to those given at Sinai, and cannot be annulled by what happened there (3:15–19). The principle established in God's promises to Abraham linked righteousness with faith, and had nothing to do with law; rather, the righteous person would *live on the basis of faith* (3:11). The law, however, laid down that those who obeyed its commandments must *live by them* – and made no reference to faith (v. 12). Since scripture said that righteousness belonged to those who lived by faith – not to those who lived by the works of the law – obedience to the commandments was *not* necessary for righteousness. For gentile Christians to commit themselves to obeying the commandments was not merely to adopt an out-of-date-system, but was to put their trust in the wrong thing.

Because of his agitated response to this situation, Paul's attitude to the law in Galatians seems very negative. The law is a custodian, exercising discipline over the Jews (3:22–4). It has brought a curse (3:10). But it is not *wholly* negative. For though Paul bases his argument in part on the Galatians' experience of the Spirit, it is also based to a large extent on his interpretation of scripture. Paul does not deny the validity of what is set out in scripture, and in his arguments about the role of the Torah he appeals repeatedly to Torah itself. So in Galatians 4:21 he insists: 'Tell me, you who wish to put yourselves under the law, will you not listen to the law?' But clearly Paul no longer regards the law as the ultimate authority: rather, he sees it now as a witness to something greater.

It was not, then, that God had changed his mind, or introduced a *new* idea into his plan. What had happened in Christ, declared Paul, was the fulfilment of his promises to Abraham. The principle linking righteousness to faith was part of his original covenant with Abraham. When Paul's opponents told the Galatians that in order to become true children of Abraham they must accept circumcision and obey all the commandments of the law they were clearly mistaken, for the *true* children of Abraham were those who shared his faith – as the law itself declares.

Paul believed, then, that he was upholding the principles set out in the Torah itself. But we can well understand why his fellow-Jews would accuse him of attacking Torah, and of seeking to undermine and destroy it! He answers such accusations in Romans, where his argument once again frequently depends on an appeal to scripture. It is true that he is arguing that the law has failed to produce righteousness, but this does not mean that he is accusing God of being unfaithful to his promises (3:3–4). When, in 3:21, he says that God's righteousness has been revealed *apart from law,* he goes on to insist that his argument is not undermining Torah but upholding it (v. 31). Then, once again appealing to what scripture says (4:3), he returns to the case of Abraham, arguing that those who maintain that his heirs need to keep the law are in fact undermining the *promise* made to Abraham – the promise which was, of course, *included* in 'the law' (4:14).

Although Romans 7 demonstrates the failure of the law – because of human weakness – to prevent sin, Paul insists that it is holy and good (v. 12). Nevertheless, it is hardly surprising if he feels the need to return to the question of the role of the law in Romans chapters 9–10. It is part of a wider problem – that of Israel herself, to whom God had entrusted many privileges, including the law (9:1–5), yet who has rejected the gospel. Paul insists that God's word has *not* failed (9:6), and argues that Israel has failed to understand the principle that links righteousness with faith. Because they had thought that righteousness belonged to those who kept the works of the law, they had misunderstood God's promises (9:30–10:13). However, because God himself is faithful to his promises, he has *not* rejected his people (11:1) and will finally save them all (11:11–36).

In Romans, therefore, Paul accuses his fellow-Jews of misunderstanding the law's purpose (9:30–10:13). When the law is understood as command, its result is to *lead* men and women into sin (Rom. 7:7–20). But the purpose of the law was *not* to show men and women how they could achieve righteousness by obeying its commands; rather it was to witness to the righteousness that God bestows through faith (Rom. 3:21). By his constant appeals to scripture – that is, to the law itself – Paul attempts to show that the real purpose of the law is to point men and women to the revelation of God's righteousness in Christ.

We see, then, how it is that Paul can maintain that he is not undermining the law but upholding its authority. As a loyal Jew, he cannot deny that God revealed himself to Moses and to the prophets. As a former Pharisee, trained in the interpretation of scripture, his arguments depend on the way in which key passages in the law and the prophets are understood. As a Christian, he understands all scripture to be pointing forward to Christ.

Christ: the goal of the law

When Paul declares that 'Christ is the end of the law' in Romans 10:4, therefore, he cannot mean that the law has been overthrown. Like our word 'end', the Greek term *telos* can mean both 'abolition' *and* 'fulfilment'; both 'full stop' *and* 'goal'. There has been heated discussion among commentators as to which meaning the term has here, but the logic of Paul's position means that its primary meaning must be 'fulfilment' or 'goal'. But, of course, when something reaches its fulfilment, its role is complete, and so it reaches its end in the sense of 'termination'. When students studying for a degree pass their final examinations, they receive their degree certificates as a symbol of the fact that their studies have achieved their goal. They no longer need to attend the lectures or write the essays designed for the course that they have completed. The course of studies that they have been pursuing has come to its end, not because it has been shown to be false or inadequate, but because its purpose has been achieved. In the same way, once runners in a marathon have reached the finishing tape, they do not have to rerun the course, because they have obtained their goal. This is Paul's logic regarding the law. Of course it was good and holy, since it was given to Israel by God, but its goal – righteousness – has been reached, the gracious gift of God in Christ, and the law's work is done. There is certainly no need for Gentiles to obey its rules. And Jews must beware lest they misunderstand the law's role, and lose sight of its goal.[9]

The idea that Christ is the *goal* of the law confirms our understanding that Paul sees the *purpose* of the law as the witness to what God planned to do through him; the purpose of a journey is to arrive at one's goal. If the law witnesses to Christ, then Christ is clearly greater than the law. For Judaism, however, the law was the supreme self-revelation of God, and the embodiment of his glory. Exodus tells us that when God spoke to Moses on Sinai, Moses was allowed to glimpse a part of God's glory – that is, he was allowed to comprehend something of what God was like (Exod. 33:18–23). The result was that Moses himself reflected God's glory to such an extent that, like a radioactive substance, he became dangerous to others (Exod. 34:29–35)! In 2 Corinthians 3, Paul uses this story to compare the glory of the Torah with that which Christians see in Christ: naturally, he claims that the latter is far greater. That, of course, is because he believes that God has revealed himself fully in Christ, whereas his revelation in the law was partial and temporary (2 Cor. 3:7–4:6). The reason that Christ's glory is greater than that of the Torah is that he is 'the image of God' – the fullest possible revelation of his glory (4:4). At the beginning of creation, God said 'let there be light', and that light shone again on Sinai, when God spoke to Moses and revealed his glory to him; but Christ is God's definitive word, and the full revelation of the light of his glory (4:6).

The use of the word 'end' to translate *telos* in Romans 10:4 can too easily suggest a change of plan, as though God had abandoned one course of action and decided to try another. This, we have argued, is *not* what Paul means! The God of Israel does not change (Mal. 3:6), and his name, Yahweh,[10] is said to mean 'I am who I am', suggesting constancy (Exod. 3:14). Paul himself insists that God is faithful – unlike men and women, who continually change their minds (2 Cor. 1:17–18). The word 'goal', on the other hand, suggests something that had been part of God's intention from the very beginning. Jewish tradition spoke of the law as having been in the mind of God – or 'pre-existent' – and this is clearly what Paul is claiming for Christ. The glory Moses glimpsed on Mount Sinai was the glory of the Lord, now seen in the face of Christ. He is the image of God (2 Cor. 4:4) – the pattern after which Adam was, according to the creation narrative, fashioned (Gal. 1:26). He, rather than the law, is the embodiment of God's will and purpose.

It is ideas like this which lie behind the 'hymn' which extols Christ in Colossians 1:15–20. Whether or not this was written by Paul himself, it certainly explores the implications of what he says in earlier letters. Its language reflects what is said in Jewish wisdom literature about Wisdom, a figure who personifies the wisdom or word of God, and so is identified with both the word by which he created the world and the word which he spoke to Moses in the law (e.g. Sirach 24:23). In 2 Corinthians, Paul linked the glory of Christ, who is God's image (4:4), not simply with Sinai (3:7–18), but with creation (4:6). In Colossians 1:15, Christ is again identified as the image of the invisible God, by whom (in whom and through whom) all things were created (1:16–17), and by whom (in whom and through whom) all things have now been reconciled to God (1:18–20). *Christ* is God's sole agent – both of creation *and* of his purpose for men and women, which is now being worked out in the Church.[11]

What Judaism claimed for the law, then, Paul is now claiming for Christ. God had indeed revealed his glory in the law, but this was only a reflection of his full glory, now seen in Christ. But because the Torah itself reflects God's glory – though in a limited way – Paul had no difficulty in appealing to it when discussing ethical issues. Since Christ is the goal of the law, life 'in Christ' or 'in the Spirit' is the fulfilment of the law's commands (Rom. 8:4; 13:8–10; Gal. 5:14; 6:2). It is no accident that Paul spells out this fulfilment of the law in terms of *love* (cf. 1 Corinthians 13). Love of

God and neighbour is a uniting force, that brings men and women together (1 Corinthians 12–14). Life *under the law,* however, in spite of requiring love of God and neighbour, had in effect separated the Jews from others, since the commandment prescribing circumcision, the observance of the sabbath, and the careful practice of food-laws – the very things that marked them out as God's people – had in fact distinguished them from other nations.

Some modern commentators have accused Paul of being inconsistent in his teaching on the law.[12] To some of his contemporaries, also, he may well have appeared so. Certainly some of his converts seem to have found his teaching confusing, for on the one hand, he insisted that they must not subject themselves to the law, while on the other, he appealed to the law – e.g. when it spoke of love – and reflected its teaching in his attitudes to sexual behaviour; moreover, he seems to have expected Gentiles to understand his frequent references to scripture, and so to be familiar with the law itself. It is hardly surprising, then, if some of them assumed that they should take other teaching in the Torah seriously, and follow that also.

But standing where he stood, Paul was entirely consistent. As a Jew, he continued to believe that the God who called Israel and who revealed himself to Abraham, Moses and the prophets was faithful. But as a Christian, the understanding he had previously had of the role of the law had been turned on its head, and this meant that he had been forced to rethink the role of the law. The fact that he had discovered something even better than Torah does not mean that what he had previously prized had been *useless at the time.* Like an enthusiastic salesman describing the merits of a new washing-powder, he insists that one packet of the new product is worth far more than two packets of his company's previous formula. Yet only the previous week that same salesman had been singing the praises of the old product! For Paul, of course, there was far more difference between the law and Christ than between two versions of a washing-powder – but there is one essential parallel between the two comparisons. Just as the two washing-powders come from the same manufacturer, so both Torah and Christ are revelations of the same God. There is continuity as well as discontinuity. Once again we can adapt our diagram representing life in the two ages:

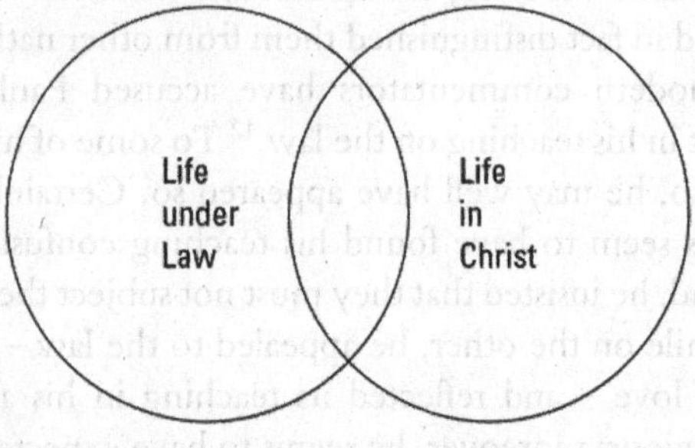

Because Paul's argument about the role of the law was part of a heated debate carried out in a particular set of circumstances, it was misunderstood later, when the problem of what should be demanded of gentile converts was no longer an issue. Paul had necessarily stressed the superiority of the new to the old and the benefits of living 'in the Spirit' to living 'under the law', because he did not wish the Gentiles to take a retrograde step. Life under the law was no longer an appropriate way of life for Christians. But because the circumstances in which Paul had attacked 'life under law' were forgotten, his words came to be seen as an attack on the law itself. In spite of his protestations to the contrary, later interpreters saw him as overturning the law (Rom. 3:31). Taken out of their original context, his condemnation of those who advocated life under the law was used as fuel for anti-Semitism. Prejudice and fear exploited what he appeared to say, distorting his words and producing suspicion, enmity, hatred and persecution. The tragic results were built on a misunderstanding of Paul's arguments, and are a travesty of the gospel which Paul proclaimed – the gospel of grace for all.

8

'The gospel concerning God's son'

Central to Paul's message was his belief that Christ had died 'for us', and had been raised from the dead. What did he mean by that 'for us'? In some places he amplifies its meaning: Christ died – or was 'handed over' – 'for our trespasses' (Rom. 4:25) or 'for our sins' (1 Cor. 15:3; Gal. 1:3). His death is specifically linked with human sin. Why? This is a problem that Paul attempts to explain when he spells out his understanding of the significance of the gospel in Romans.

Universal sin

Jewish tradition saw death as the punishment for sin. Not only were criminals put to death, but the fact that all living creatures are condemned to die was explained as the result of Adam's sin. According to the story in Genesis 3, Adam and Eve were expelled from the Garden of Eden lest they take and eat the fruit of the tree of life (Gen. 3:22). Death was understood to be the universal punishment for human sin, but it was universal, not simply as the result of Adam's action, but because his descendants *shared* his sin (2 Esdras 3:21–2, 25–6; 7:48 (118)). As we have seen, the hope of future deliverance for God's people came in time to include the hope of everlasting life (Dan. 12:1–3).

Jesus had died a violent death, and the manner of his death proclaimed him a transgressor (Deut. 21:23). It was certainly not the kind of death one would have thought appropriate for

God's Messiah![1] Before his conversion, Paul had assumed that the manner of his death was clear evidence that Jesus was *not* the Messiah, but now that he believed that he *was,* how was he to explain his death? Could it be that the death of the Messiah – the representative of the nation – was the sign of God's judgement on his people? Notwithstanding the privileges they had received – including the Torah – they had been found wanting, and in the judgement pronounced on Jesus, they themselves were condemned (Rom. 8:3).[2]

It is important to remember that Paul began from what was 'given' – in this case, the fact that Jesus, whom he now believed to be the Messiah, had died a criminal's death – and had to make sense of that. Given this totally unexpected event, he was forced to ask the question 'Why?' In seeking to answer that question, he naturally drew on his Jewish beliefs about sin and about the love and mercy of God. He did *not* begin from any expectation that the Messiah would be put to death.

There was, however, another important element in what was 'given', and which therefore needed to be explained, and this was the resurrection (Rom. 1:4). If death signified judgement and condemnation, resurrection signified approval and acquittal. Nor was it Jesus alone who had been 'justified' by his resurrection, since there were clear signs that others had been justified too: Christians now enjoyed peace with God (Rom. 5:1), and the Holy Spirit had been poured out on them (Rom. 8:9). If the death of the Messiah signified the condemnation of all God's people, his resurrection signified their restoration. Paul sums up what he understands to have happened in two lines at the end of Romans 4, where he says that God raised 'Jesus our Lord'

> who was handed over [to death] for our trespasses,
> and was raised for our acquittal.[3]

So far, this reasoning might suggest that Israel's sins had been dealt with, and that those Jews who responded to the gospel had experienced this restoration. But we already know that Paul's conviction that the law had failed to give the life it promised, together with his discovery that Gentiles were experiencing the gift of the Spirit, had persuaded him that both Jews *and* Gentiles could be members of the new community. God is the God of Gentiles, as well as of Jews, and he deals with both in the same way (Rom. 3:27–31). In Romans he sets out to argue this case logically, and we must therefore trace his argument there.

First, he shows how everyone, Jew and Gentile alike, has sinned; because they have all failed to give glory to God (Rom. 1:23), they have lost the glory of God which Adam reflected before his fall (Rom. 3:23). There are intriguing echoes of Adam's story in the description of human sin in Romans 1:18–32,[4] underlining Paul's point that sin is a universal phenomenon. Although Israel had been given the law, she had failed to keep it, and so God had dealt with sin in the death of Christ, *apart from* the law (Romans 3:21–6). This means that there is one way and one way only to become righteous, and that is by trusting in what God has done through Christ's death (Rom. 3:27–31).

God's righteousness

In what way, then, does Paul understand the death of Christ to have dealt with sin? He explains in Romans 3:21–6. What has happened, he says, is that God has revealed his righteousness, as the Jewish scriptures, both law and prophets, witnessed that he would (Rom. 3:21, picking up 1:17). In the Old Testament, the Hebrew word for 'righteousness', *s-d-q,* means 'right-ness', and so sets the standard to which one should conform; whatever is righteous conforms to this standard. Since God himself is righteous, he can be relied upon to act rightly, and because he is the judge of all the earth, he will reward the righteous and punish the wicked. When God reveals his righteousness, therefore, it means that he puts things straight, sets them to rights. From the point of view of those who had endeavoured to remain faithful to God, this setting of things to rights seems to promise their 'justification' – the recognition that they are righteous – and their deliverance from their enemies. Hence the word 'righteousness' is almost synonymous in some passages with 'salvation'.[5] For the wicked, however, this revelation of righteousness will mean wrath (Rom. 1:18). The idea that God might 'justify' the ungodly (Rom. 4:5) is clearly preposterous. And yet this is precisely what Paul is now claiming has happened.

One of our problems in trying to understand Paul's thought is the fact that Greek words do not necessarily correspond with English ones. In this case, we have an added problem, since English is deficient. In Greek there is a series of clearly related words, all of which are concerned with the idea of what is right: *dikaiosunē* (a noun, meaning 'righteousness'), *dikaios* (an adjective, 'righteous'), *dikaiōs* (an adverb, 'rightly'), *dikaiōma* (a noun, meaning 'right command' or 'right action'), together with a noun, *dikaiōsis,* and a verb, *dikaioō,* that clearly belong to the same group. In English we have the noun 'righteousness' (though this has a somewhat static meaning, rather than the active sense, which is close to the word 'salvation'), the adjective 'righteous', and the adverbs 'righteously' and 'rightly'; but when it comes to using a verb with the same stem ('right'), we have no verb 'to righteous', and in order to translate *dikaioō,* we therefore have to use a phrase such as 'to set things to rights'; as for the Greek noun *dikaiōsis,* this has to be translated 'acquittal', even though it has the same stem as the other terms. We do have an alternative set of terms available in English, however, and these are the nouns 'justice' and 'justification' (for the active sense), the adjective 'just', adverb 'justly', and the verb 'to justify'. These words have the advantage that they remind us that righteousness concerns one's relationship with other human beings: in other words, it includes what we would term 'social justice'. Love of God cannot be separated from love of neighbour. But here, too, there are problems. All these terms suggest legal rights rather than ethical goodness, a legal status rather than right attitudes, and though that is one aspect of the meaning of these words, it is not the whole story. This set of words has the advantage that it supplies us with a verb 'to justify', but this is rarely used today except when we request a computer to justify the margins (a reminder that it originally meant 'to bring into conformity with') and when politicians set out to justify their own questionable actions – which they do by launching a verbal defence, not by putting things right!

There is clearly no totally satisfactory solution. We have preferred to use the set of words based on 'righteous'. For the verb, instead of 'to justify', we shall in future use the simple 'to right', a verb which normally means 'to restore to the proper position' (as with a boat) but can also mean to vindicate or avenge (as in righting wrongs), to rehabilitate or put right.

Paul claims that the righteousness of God – that is, his salvation – which the law and the prophets had promised would be demonstrated, has now been revealed. But it has been revealed *apart from* the law, and not on the basis of whether or not one has kept the law (Rom. 3:21), and it is therefore effective for all who have faith (v. 22). All human beings need to be righted, since all have sinned (v. 23). Things have been put right as a sheer gift by the grace of God, 'through the redemption which is in Christ Jesus' (v. 24). God set him forth as a *hilasterion,* explains Paul, by means of his death. We shall look at the meaning of this Greek word in a moment. Meanwhile, we notice that God is said to have done this in order to show his righteousness, because he had passed over sins up to this point (and therefore had to deal with them, v. 25). This was, Paul insists again, to show his righteousness, so that he himself might be righteous, and so that he might right the person who has faith (v. 26).

This short paragraph is packed with theological dynamite. Paul's fellow-Jews would have been shocked by its opening words: 'But now, *apart from* law . . .' The notion that God's righteousness might be displayed on some other basis would have been abhorrent to them. Yet this revelation was witnessed to by law and prophets: Paul insists on the continuity between past and present.

God's righteousness is offered to all who believe, says Paul, but the basis on which this is done is the grace of God. This time, Paul's fellow-Jews would have been in agreement. God's righteousness and his grace, or mercy, overlapped. It is interesting to compare a passage from the Community Document, one of the scrolls found at Qumran:[6]

> I acknowledge his judgement concerning my sins
> and my transgressions shall be before my eyes as an engraved decree.
> I will say to God 'My righteousness',
> and 'Author of my well-being'.
>
> (1 QS X: 11–12)

This document, probably written about 100 BC, acknowledges human sin – even in a community devoted to obeying his law – and expresses dependence on God. The theme is repeated in the next column:

> As for me, my judgement is with God.
> In his hand are the perfection of my way
> and the uprightness of my heart.
> He will wipe out my transgression
> through his righteousness . . .
> As for me, I belong to wicked mankind,
> and to the company of ungodly flesh . . .
> For mankind has no way,
> and man is unable to establish his steps
> since judgement is with God
> and perfection of way is from his hand . . .

As for me, if I stumble, the mercies of God
shall be my eternal salvation.
If I stagger because of the sin of flesh,
my judgement shall be
by the righteousness of God which endures for ever . . .

He will draw me near by his grace,
and by his mercy will he bring my judgement.
He will judge me in the righteousness of his truth,
and in the greatness of his goodness
He will pardon all my sins.
Through his righteousness he will cleanse me
of the uncleanness of man
and of the sins of the children of men,
that I may confess to God his righteousness,
and his majesty to the Most High.

(1 QS XI:2–3, 9–10, 12, 13–15)[7]

What the author of this key-document used by the Qumran community said about sins and about relying on God's righteousness and mercy is very close to what Paul says. The one thing the former would not have said, however, is that God's righteousness operates *apart from* law.

God's righteousness has been revealed in the redemption that is in Christ Jesus (Rom. 3:24). The original meaning of the English verb 'to redeem', like that of the Greek verb behind it, was 'to buy back' – i.e. to recover something one had previously owned which had passed into someone else's possession (as in redeeming a pledge from the pawnbroker); it was commonly used of the freeing of a slave, when that slave – or someone acting on his behalf – bought his freedom. Paul would have been familiar with both verb and noun, since they were used in the Septuagint, the Greek version of the Old Testament, to describe God's action in redeeming Israel from slavery in Egypt at the Exodus (e.g. Deut. 7:8); they had been used again by prophets who longed for the time when God would once again 'redeem' his people by rescuing them from domination by their enemies (e.g. Isa. 52:3).

From what, then, did God, through Christ, redeem the human race? Paul has argued that all human beings are 'under' the power of sin (Rom. 3:9) and he will go on to explain that Christians are like slaves who have changed their masters (6:15–19): they are no longer slaves of sin, but slaves (as it were) of righteousness. What they are redeemed from is the power of sin.

The place of reconciliation

In verse 25, Paul uses another metaphor. Christ has been set forth by God as an *hilastērion,* through faith, by his blood (or death). Unfortunately there is considerable dispute as to the meaning of the noun *hilastērion,* as the various translations and paraphrases offered in modern versions demonstrate. Among these are 'a sacrifice of atonement' (NRSV and NIV), 'the means of expiating sin' (REB), and 'so as to win reconciliation' (JB).[8] In the Septuagint, the word means none of these things, but refers to something which had a permanent place in the holy of holies in the temple. This seems to have been positioned above the ark of the covenant, where the books of Torah were kept, and is generally referred to as 'the cover of the ark' or, since this is where God was thought to dwell and the place where reconciliation between God and his people took place, the 'seat of mercy'.[9] Once a year the high priest came into the holy of holies and sprinkled blood on the *hilastērion:* it was therefore the place where atonement was made. The scene is described in Hebrews 9:2–7.

Why, then, do our translations prefer to speak of Christ as a sacrifice, rather than as a *place* of sacrifice? There are three reasons: one is that scholars find it difficult to imagine Paul speaking of him as a piece of furniture! The second is that they object that Christ cannot be both a sacrifice (an idea implied in the phrase 'by his death') *and* the place where sacrifice is offered. They therefore understand *hilastērion* to explain the *nature* of Christ's death: by his death he became an atoning sacrifice. Justification for this interpretation is then found in the third argument, which is that in later Jewish literature, influenced by Greek ideas, the word *hilastērion* did come to be used in the sense of 'atoning sacrifice': notably, it was used in this sense of the death of the Maccabaean martyrs (4 Macc. 17:22).

Notwithstanding these objections, we have to note that the idea of Christ as *the place where God and human beings are reconciled* is a highly appropriate one for the development of Paul's argument. Nor is there any real reason why he should not have thought of Christ as both the victim and the place of sacrifice; the author of Hebrews does something similar in describing Jesus as both the high priest *and* the sacrifice which he himself offers (Heb. 9:11–14). Finally, Paul's use of the Old Testament elsewhere suggests that his ideas are probably drawn from the Old Testament image of the mercy-seat, and the way in which the word *hilastērion* is used in Exodus and Leviticus.

What the ritual connected with the mercy-seat provided was a method of dealing with those sins which – in spite of all the other sacrifices offered throughout the year – remained as a barrier between God and his people. In Paul's thought, too, it would seem that what God deals with are the sins that, in his forbearance, he has passed over; they have created a barrier between God and human beings and need to be removed. Once a year the high priest entered the holy of holies and, far from any human gaze, sprinkled blood on the mercy-seat, in order to deal with the sins that had come between God and his people. It was a very private ceremony, for the mercy-seat was hidden from public gaze. But now something very public has taken place. God has 'set forth' a new 'mercy-seat' – Christ – sprinkled with blood in the sight of all (cf. Gal. 3:1); he is the place of reconciliation, and by his death, sins have been dealt with once and for all. Since God has now dealt with sins, he is seen to be righteous; moreover, he has 'righted' all who have faith, having brought about reconciliation between himself and *all* people, not simply (as with the high priest) between himself and the Jews. Paul's use of 'set forth' and 'blood' here alongside the word *hilasterion* suggest that it is this imagery that he has in mind. The blood sprinkled on the old mercy-seat dealt with the sins of Israel; the blood of Jesus, who is himself the true 'mercy-seat', deals with the sins of the world. For God is the God of Gentiles as well as of Jews, and rights them all in the same way (Rom. 3:27–31).

What, then, does it mean to be 'righted'? Ever since the Reformation, when Martin Luther insisted that the heart of Paul's gospel was 'justification by faith', the precise meaning of the verb has been hotly debated. Luther himself argued that the imagery was that of the law-court, and that the word meant 'to declare righteous'. But how, it is asked – and why – should God declare those who are still sinners to be righteous? In contrast, it was argued that the verb must mean 'to make righteous', since God does not simply *pronounce* sinners to be righteous, but *changes* them. In other words, Paul thinks of righteousness as being *imparted* to men and women, not just *imputed*. In fact, as we shall see, there is some truth in both these views.[10] If Paul thinks of Christians as being *declared* righteous, it is because Christ himself has been declared righteous, and because those who are 'in Christ' share his status. If he thinks of them as being *made* righteous, it is because, 'in Christ', they become – or should become – like him. We shall explore these ideas later. In the meantime, we note that being 'righted' clearly involves also the idea that men and women are restored to a right relationship with God – the relationship which, according to Jewish tradition, had been lost when Adam and Eve sinned.

Paul has insisted in Romans 3:21–31 that this righteousness is bestowed on those who have faith. Now, in chapter 4, he demonstrates that this was true of Abraham, who was regarded by Jews as having been truly righteous. Paul here re-works the argument about Abraham that he had used previously in Galatians 3, showing that Abraham had faith, and did not rely on obedience to the law. The covenant between God and Abraham had been made on the basis of God's grace and Abraham's faith – *not* his 'works' (Rom. 4:1–16). The promise made to Abraham and to his descendants that he would be the father of many nations is now being fulfilled, argues Paul, since his true descendants are in fact all who have faith, and not simply his physical descendants (Rom. 4:11–25). So 'faith' – or 'trust' – is all that is required; through Christ, believers have access to their new status before God, confident that they will one day share the glory of God which they – like Adam before them – had lost because of their sin (Rom. 5:1–2).

Adam and Christ

So far in the argument, Paul has been talking in general categories, referring to 'everyone', to 'Jews' and to 'Gentiles'. Although we have detected traces of Adam's story, he has not yet been mentioned. In Romans 5:12–21 he comes out into the open for the first time, in a passage which sums up where Paul's argument has led him. What he claims here is that since the sin of Adam had universal significance – leading to universal sin and death – so, too, what God has done through Christ *also* had universal significance, reversing the effects of Adam's trespass and bringing righteousness and life for all. Instead of the condemnation that followed Adam's sin we have acquittal (v. 16), and instead of the death that ruled the world as a result of Adam's trespass, we have those who have received the free gift of righteousness 'ruling in life', as they were meant to do in God's original plan (v. 17, cf. Gen. 1:26).

Paul's comparisons here are top-heavy, and cannot be set out in any elegant rhetorical form. The reason is plain: what God has done – and is doing – in Christ is far greater than what Adam did. God's grace is more powerful than sin, and life is greater than death. So although Paul begins in verse 12 with an introductory 'just as' followed by 'so', dealing with the relationship between sin and death, the sentence is broken off; by the time he comes to the figures of Adam and Christ in verses 15–17, what we have is a series of contrasts: the gracious gift is *not* like the trespass (v. 15) and the gift is *not* like the result of one man's sin (v. 16). The result of God's grace is *much more* than the result of the trespass (vv. 15, 17). Even when Paul attempts straightforward contrasts, in verses 18–19, the first of them is not exact: as the trespass of Adam led to condemnation for all, so the acquittal of Christ led to righteousness of life for all;[11] as many were made sinners because of Adam's disobedience, so many *will* be made righteous because of Christ's obedience.

What is the basis of Paul's claim that what Adam and Christ did had an effect on others, and why should this be thought to have happened? In the case of Adam, the link between him and other human beings is clear: the name 'Adam' means 'man', and the story of the Fall was an attempt to explain why sin and death are universal experiences. That story, too, started from a 'given' – sin and death – and sought an explanation. With our modern knowledge of genes and DNA, we can easily grasp the notion that there is a common bond between us and the progenitors of the human race. The story of Adam was not intended to shift blame, however, but to explain human weakness and to acknowledge human responsibility. With our modern understanding of the interdependence of nations and societies, too, we can appreciate the belief that we all share responsibility for what takes place in the world, and we realize that we cannot detach ourselves from its problems. The price we pay for goods in one country affects the standard of living in another; the pollution created on one side of the world changes the climate on the other; trade agreements between some nations result in starvation in others. What 'Adam' does certainly affects others.

Paul, of course, treats Adam as an historical figure, but he is clearly aware of his symbolic significance. Indeed, there is a sense in which he 'demythologizes' Adam, by drawing out the meaning *behind* the story.[12] What he argues in Romans 5 is based on the claim that Christ – who is certainly an historical figure – has the same kind of significance for other human beings as does Adam. The basis of his claim must once again be Christian experience: he himself has met the Lord and is therefore convinced that Christ has been raised from the dead; he believes that his new life 'in Christ' means that Christians have been restored to the relationship with God which Adam threw away. How had righteousness and life replaced sin and death? Whereas Adam was disobedient, Christ was obedient; whereas Adam sinned, Christ was acknowledged to be righteous; whereas Adam was condemned to death, Christ was raised to life.

But what was it that enabled 'the one man Jesus Christ' to reverse what had been done by 'the one man' Adam? Paul insists that Jesus himself was descended from Adam. He was, he tells us, 'born of a woman' (Gal. 4:4), 'a descendant of David' (Rom. 1:3); he bore 'the likeness of a man' and shared our 'human form' (Phil. 2:7).[13] Indeed, he shared our human condition to such an extent that he could be said to have come 'in the likeness of sinful flesh' (Rom. 8:3), even though he did not share our sin. How had this one man been able to break free from the sin that had infected all humanity and so brought life in place of death?

A careful reading of Romans 5 reveals the answer. The reason why the comparisons and contrasts are unbalanced is, as we have already noted, that *God* is at work through 'the one man Jesus Christ'. The scales are unevenly balanced because *God* has intervened, pressing down on the side of Christ: it is the grace of God, and his gifts, that are at work in Christ (5:15–16); the great reverse has come about because God gave up his Son and raised him from the dead. This does not mean, of course, that Jesus is a mere puppet: rather, he is God's Son, fully obedient to God's will, and so the channel through whom God is at work. Paul sums it up in Romans 8:3, where he says that what has been done has been done by 'God, sending his Son in the likeness of sinful flesh'. Jesus was the one man who was able to break free from Adam's legacy – because, and only because, he was also Son of God.

In the case of Adam, the link between him and other human beings was obvious. But Paul apparently sees 'the one man Jesus Christ' as the beginning of a new humanity, and those who belong to this new humanity are enabled to conform once again to the plan which God had for them at creation. What is the link between Christ and those who are enabled to share *his* experience? Paul endeavours to explain this in Romans 6.

Christians should no longer be living the old kind of life of sin that belonged to Adam's descendants (Rom. 6:1). The reason is that they have been baptized 'into' Christ. As a result, they are able to share his experiences. When Christ was put to death, his life as a child of Adam came to its end – he died to the old life, which was limited, as Paul puts it, by 'the weakness of flesh'. His resurrection inaugurated a new way of life – the life of the Spirit. The bridge between old and new came with the death and resurrection of Christ, who shared human life 'in Adam' in order to inaugurate the new life 'in Christ'. Seen from *this* angle, our overlapping ages look like this:

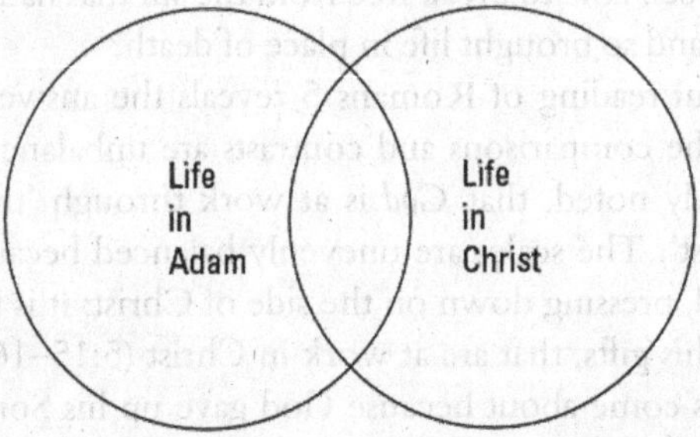

In order to share in this new kind of experience, therefore – what Paul terms life 'in Christ', in contrast to the life which is in reality death 'in Adam' (1 Cor. 15:22) – it is necessary to share the experience which brought Christ himself there: in other words, it is necessary to die with Christ and to be raised with him (Rom. 6:3–11). In so doing, human beings die to the life which is dominated by sin, and receive the righteousness which leads to life (Rom. 5:18, 21).

Paul's language was not only striking but shocking. The only way to share the new life of the new age was apparently to share Christ's death – and even the manner of his death, for in Romans 6:6 he gives extra force to the metaphor of 'dying with Christ' by describing how the old self[14] has been '*crucified with* Christ' (cf. Gal. 2:19). The verb 'to crucify with' drives home the radical nature of the change in a believer's life. Crucifixion, as we have already noted, was a cruel and shameful death. This is no gentle progression, but a clear break with the past, and one demanding considerable self-sacrifice: the life that is offered must indeed be worth pursuing if this is the cost that has to be paid!

The language is, of course, metaphorical: Paul is certainly not advocating the philosophy of a suicide cult. Christians continue to live in this world, and must therefore, inevitably, expect to die. Paul speaks of 'dying with Christ' in order to emphasize the radical break which *should* have taken place in the lives of believers, who ought no longer to be living in the way that 'Adam' lived. But since they continue to be limited by physical constraints (what Paul calls 'the flesh'), resurrection remains a future hope. For this reason, although Paul speaks of Christians dying with Christ as a *past* experience, he speaks of rising with Christ as a *future* one (Rom. 6:5–11). Nevertheless, the new life that comes with Christ's resurrection is experienced already by those who have shared his death. 'Newness of life' is seen in their behaviour (Rom. 6:4), and Christians must think of themselves as having died to sin, and living now for God (Rom. 6:11). Like slaves who have been bought and sold, they have, in effect, changed masters (Rom. 6:15–23).

There is, then, an obvious difference between that which links men and women to Adam, and that which links them to Christ.

Whereas they share in the experience of Adam whether they wish to or not, sharing in the experience of Christ comes about through a deliberate identification with his death and resurrection. This takes place in baptism, and the image Paul uses in Romans 6:4 – 'we have been buried with him by baptism into death' – suggests that in his day Christians were baptized by being submerged in running water (cf. Acts 8:36–9; 16:13–15). Indeed, the verb *baptizō* means to submerge, not to sprinkle. Going down into the waters and coming up from beneath them provided an obvious symbol for death and resurrection.

In Christ

But how is it that men and women are able to identify themselves with Christ's death and resurrection? *How* are they able to 'die to sin' as he did (Rom. 6:2, 10) and to share his risen life? There are two areas of Paul's thought that we need to explore in order to answer these questions.

First, we need to note that in comparing Adam with Christ, Paul referred to each of them as 'the one man' (Rom. 5:12, 15, 19). In 5:14, he described Adam as a 'type' of the one to come. The Greek word *typos,* like its English equivalent, can mean a pattern, but it has other meanings too: a copy of an original, an impression made by a die (and so the *reverse* of the original), or that die itself. The one man Adam was scarcely a 'pattern' for the one man Christ – except in respect of the influence which each of them had on others – and the contrasts Paul draws between them suggests that the image he has in mind is that of 'type' and 'antitype'. Adam and Christ stand in contrast to each other because Adam was the reverse of what man was intended to be, and Christ was their *true* pattern. Elsewhere, Paul speaks of Christ as 'the image of God' (2 Cor. 4:4; cf. Col. 1:15), and he describes how Christians are expected to bear Christ's image (Rom. 8:29; 1 Cor. 15:49; 2 Cor. 3:18; Col. 3:10). Adam, we are told in Genesis 1:26, was created 'after the image of God'. But Adam was a flawed copy of that image, whereas Christ is the authentic pattern of our humanity. As such, he is the one with whose death and resurrection men and women may identify.

Secondly, we should take note of Paul's favourite expression 'in Christ', a phrase that he uses repeatedly throughout his letters. The phrase strikes us as an odd one, for there is no parallel, either in ancient literature or in the modern world. However much we may identify ourselves with the objectives of a political leader, sympathize with the philosophy of a particular guru, or be carried away by the performance of a pop singer, we would not describe ourselves as 'in' that particular person.

Paul himself *does* supply two parallels, however. In 1 Corinthians 15:22, his conviction that 'all will be made alive in Christ' stands in contrast to the statement that 'all die in Adam', while earlier in that epistle, in 1 Corinthians 10:2, he describes the Israelites as having all been 'baptized into Moses'. Both statements seem to have been coined by analogy with those he makes about Christ, but they provide us with some clues as to the meaning of the phrase 'in Christ'.

To understand 1 Corinthians 15:22, we need to look at the parallel statement in verse 21:

> Since death [came] through a man,
> so also the resurrection of the dead [comes] through a man.

The 'in Adam' and the 'in Christ' in verse 22 could, in fact, be translated 'by Adam' and 'by Christ', making the parallel between the verses even clearer, since the Greek preposition *en* (like its Hebrew equivalent) means 'by' as well as 'in'. Both verses 21 and 22 make the point that we live because of what Christ did, just as we die because of what Adam did. Nevertheless, the 'in' in verse 22 serves to remind us of our close relationship with both Adam and Christ. The story of Adam is understood as a story about all human beings, and Adam is seen in solidarity with his descendants. We may contrast the Greek myth about Pandora, who opened a box and let loose all manner of ills upon the earth: men and women could blame her, without sharing her responsibility. Adam is seen as a representative figure in a way that Pandora was not.

1 Corinthians 10:2 is part of an argument in which Paul reminds the Corinthians that they cannot simply rely on their baptism into Christ for salvation: dying and rising with Christ, as we shall see, is not a once-in-a-lifetime event, but a continuing experience. The comparison that Paul is making here is not with Adam but with Moses, since Paul detects a tendency in the church which was present also in Israel. The Jews had often assumed that, because they were God's special people, he would save them: they relied on the fact that, through Moses, God had given them his law. The notion of being 'baptized into Moses' is a strange one, probably inspired by the story of the passage through the Red Sea, but 'Moses' was a synonym for the Torah, and both the manna and the water miraculously supplied to Israel in the wilderness (vv. 3–4) were interpreted as symbols of Torah.[15] The law had appeared to promise life to those who obeyed it – so reversing the effects of Adam's fall – and the eschatological hope was that the righteous in Israel who obeyed the law would finally receive this life (4 Esdras 7:3–25). For Paul, however, it is life 'in Christ', not life under the Law – or 'in Moses' – that stands in contrast to life in Adam. Moses – like Adam and Christ – is a representative figure, but only because he was the one through whom God spoke to his people: 'baptism into Moses' is a symbol for 'allegiance to the law'.

What Paul understands by being 'in Christ', then, is *solidarity*, a sharing in experience. It involves a relationship not only to Christ, but to everyone else who is part of the community of those who are 'in Christ'. Unlike Moses, Christ is a figure of universal significance, since he is parallel to – and greater than – Adam himself.

It is because Christ is 'the last Adam', as he terms him in 1 Corinthians 15:45, and embodies the true pattern of what humanity should be, that human beings are able to identify themselves with his death to sin and to share his risen life.

In Romans 7, Paul deals with the inability of the law to deal with the human predicament, a problem that he has already referred to (Rom. 2:17–3:20) but not yet explained. The law was rendered powerless, he now argues, because of the weakness of the flesh – a weakness that has been demonstrated in the story of Adam. Yet what the law was unable to do, God has now achieved, by sending his Son as a human being to deal with sin (8:3). How? Paul says two things here about Christ's coming. First, he came as a human being – literally, 'in the likeness of sinful flesh'; i.e. he shared fully in what it meant to be a child of Adam. Secondly, he came to deal with sin – literally, 'for sin'. In Greek these two words were sometimes used in the Septuagint to translate the Hebrew word meaning 'sin-offering', since this sacrifice was offered 'for sin'. Does Paul have that idea in mind here?

That is possible. If so, then once again, as in Romans 3:25, we have an attempt to explain how God dealt with sin (cf. 4:25a). But the emphasis is on the result: sin has been condemned 'in the flesh', but Christians now live 'in the Spirit'. The *purpose* of Christ's coming was that the law's requirement for righteousness might be fulfilled in those who are joined to Christ. Paul does not claim that he has done anything to meet the law's requirement for righteousness, only that this requirement has been met by God's action in sending his Son. God sent his Son in human form, *so that* it might be fulfilled in us. By Christ's identification with sinful humanity, and by his condemnation of sin, he enables those who share his death and resurrection to share his righteousness.

The central theme of Romans 8 is Christians' future hope. Once again, this is founded on what God has already done. He *has* raised Christ from the dead, and therefore he *will* give life to those who are mortal (8:11; cf. 5:10). Confirmation of this hope is seen in the fact that Christians have received the Spirit, and that this Spirit is at work in their lives.

Future resurrection depends, then, on the resurrection of Christ himself, and on Christians' union with him: 'Christ is in you', he tells the Romans (8:10). What happened to Christ will happen to them, and the guarantee of this is the Spirit working in them. The gift of the Spirit witnesses to the fact that they are God's children, and so heirs of all that God has in store for them. Now we realize that the consequence of God sending his Son in human form is that men and women have received adoption (Rom. 8:14–17).

But the gift of the Spirit means that Christians are *already* experiencing resurrection life; because of the righteousness that has been given them in Christ, the Spirit gives them life (Rom. 8:10). In 8:4–13, Paul contrasts what he calls 'living according to the flesh' with 'living according to the Spirit'. Those who live in the former way are those whose lives are dominated by sin and death – the result of Adam's fall – while those who live 'according to the Spirit' are those who are 'in Christ'. He presses the point home by contrasting the Spirit of God – described here as a spirit of adoption – with the spirit of slavery – i.e. to sin and death. Paul has already argued that Christ's death was a redemption (i.e. from slavery, 3:24), and that Christians who have died with Christ are no longer slaves to sin, which leads to death (Rom. 6:5–23). Now he reminds the Romans what that means: because, in Christ, they are God's children, they can expect to regain the 'glory' lost by Adam, the glory that belongs to those who are in a right relationship with God (Rom. 8:17–18). Creation itself, argues Paul, is longing for the time when this will happen; the reason is that creation was 'subjected to futility' as the result of Adam's sin (vv. 19–22). Until that happens there is tension, a tension that is experienced by Christians who wait for their *final* adoption and redemption (v. 23). In this interim period, characterized by hope (v. 24), redemption and adoption are already experienced and still awaited.

Their future hope, then, is certain, but it is not the kind of 'hope' we entertain when we say that we hope for fine weather, or hope to scoop the top prize in a charity draw! It is certain because God has called them, and it is his plan to conform them to the image of his Son – i.e. to make them like him (vv. 28–9).

Their destiny is so certain that Paul can describe it as though it were already complete: they are already 'righted', already 'glorified' (v. 30).

Paul sums up the argument in this section by reminding his readers once again of what God has done:

> He did not spare his own Son,
> but gave him up for us all.

Christians can therefore be confident about the future. If God is *for* us, argues Paul, it does not matter who is against us (vv. 31–2). The scene is now that of the Last Judgement. Who will lay a charge against God's people? Certainly not God himself, since he rights them. Who will condemn them? Certainly not Christ, who died and was raised, and stands at God's right hand, interceding on their behalf (vv. 33–4). Paul has used this kind of argument earlier, when he assured his readers that if God has righted us through Christ's death, he will save us, through him, from wrath – and again, that if we have been reconciled to God through the death of his Son, we shall certainly be saved by his life (Rom. 5:8–11). Now he concludes this section in a paean of praise to God, because nothing can separate Christians from his love, or from the love of Christ Jesus their Lord (vv. 35–9).

In the next three chapters of Romans, Paul picks up the problem of Israel's rejection of the Messiah, and argues that God has not rejected his people and that he remains faithful to his promises. Eventually they, too, will receive mercy and 'all Israel will be saved' (11:26). In spite of Israel's present failure to respond to the gospel, Paul insists that God's purpose for her will not be frustrated.

It is notable that when Paul turns to what we may call the ethical application of his gospel in chapter 12 and following, he grounds his appeal in his theological argument: 'I appeal to you, therefore . . .' His appeal is based on the mercies of God, which he has described in the previous eleven chapters. His readers are to present themselves to God 'as a living sacrifice', for in this way they will offer true worship to God – a worship that is acceptable to him (12:1). They must not be conformed to this age (i.e. the age dominated by sin), but must be transformed by the renewal of their minds, so that they discern the will of God – that which is good and acceptable and perfect (v. 2).

It is worth noting that the theme and language here are reminiscent of what was said in chapter 1, where Paul described men and women's failure to worship God, and the result was that they were given over to an 'undiscerning mind' (1:28), incapable of distinguishing good from evil. Now, because of what God has done in Christ, the community of those who live 'in Christ' should be living as God intended, honouring and praising him in their lives.

We have traced Paul's argument in Romans because it demonstrates the central place that Christ's death and resurrection occupy in Paul's understanding of God's redemption of the human race from sin and death. His argument is set against the background of world history – its beginning in the Garden of Eden, its turning point in Christ's death and resurrection, and its end on the Day of Judgement – the eschatological framework that he inherited and adapted from Judaism.

Within the argument of Romans, 3:21–6 clearly occupies a pivotal place. Yet what Paul says about Christ's death in this passage is often said by commentators to differ from the way he explains it elsewhere: certainly some of the vocabulary he uses is different. As a result, it is often concluded that he has 'borrowed' verses 25–6 from an earlier Christian statement. We have seen, however, that the section fits well into the overall argument of Romans, chapters 1–8. We must return to this problem later, when we have looked at other passages where Paul attempts to explain the significance of the death and resurrection of Christ for the human race.

9

'Christ died . . . and was raised'

There is no doubt that Christ's death and resurrection formed the central core of Paul's gospel. 'When I came to you', he writes to the Corinthians, 'I determined to know nothing among you except Jesus Christ – and him crucified' (1 Cor. 2:1–2). Yet his message certainly included the resurrection as well, since, as he reminds them in 1 Corinthians 15:17, 'if Christ has not been raised, your faith is futile'. Later theological interpretation of the Christian doctrine of the atonement has often tended to concentrate on Christ's death, as though that alone were important. But Paul insists that 'if Christ has not been raised . . . you are still in your sins'. If Christ had not been raised, he would not have been declared righteous and acknowledged as Lord, and there would be no new life for Christians to share.

The core of the gospel

Precisely because Christ's death and resurrection are the core theme of his gospel, Paul has no need to begin with them when writing to his churches. He has already preached his gospel to these people, and what is needed in the letters is encouragement and advice, explanation when things have been misunderstood, and rebuke when he believes that his readers have made mistakes. Only in Romans, where Paul sets out to explain his understanding of the implications of the gospel to a congregation which has not heard 'his' gospel before, does he begin at the beginning, and explain *why* Christ's death was necessary.

Nevertheless, Paul's message of Christ crucified and raised underlies *all* his letters. This alone is why he has been called to be an apostle. This alone is why there is a community of believers who live 'in Christ'. This alone is why they believe, why they have hope for the future, and why they are all called to live in love with one another. His letters are therefore full of reminders of the central theme of the gospel. Are the Thessalonians worried about what will happen on the Day of Judgement? Paul assures them that they have no need to be, since the Lord Jesus Christ died for them in order that they might live with him (1 Thess. 5:10). How, he protests, could the Galatians think that they need the law to right them in God's sight, when Christ crucified had been placarded before their eyes (Gal. 3:1)? The Corinthians, searching for wisdom and power, have clearly forgotten that the folly and weakness of God, seen in the cross, have overturned all human achievements (1 Cor. 1:18–25). They boast in their freedom, but need to remember that by their actions they may destroy the faith of other, weaker, Christians – men and women for whom Christ died (1 Cor. 8:11; cf. Rom. 14:15).

Paul's own experience of suffering is described as 'carrying within himself the dying of Jesus, in order that the life of Jesus may be seen there' (2 Cor. 4:10). In Philippians, thinking of his own situation facing possible execution, he speaks of sharing in the sufferings of Christ and becoming like him in his death – in hope of attaining resurrection (Phil. 3:10–11). His appeal to the Philippians to obey his teaching echoes his words about Christ's own obedience to death (2:12, 8). Their reward will be to share the glory which was given to Christ when he was exalted after death (3:20–1; 2:9–11); those who do not follow this teaching 'live as enemies of the cross of Christ' (3:18).

From time to time, in the course of his letters, these 'reminders' are given in pithy, memorable summaries of the gospel. Among these are many of the summaries that scholars tend to assume are 'pre-Pauline'. It seems more likely that they are summaries of Paul's own teaching. Whatever their origin, they are important indications of Paul's core beliefs.

Perhaps the earliest of these summaries is found in 1 Thessalonians 5:10. Paul here reminds the Thessalonians that they are destined for salvation, and not for wrath. The grounds for this belief have already been touched on in 1 Thessalonians 1:9–10, where Paul has reminded them of their initial response to his preaching. They had, he says, 'turned to God from idols, to serve a living and true God and to wait for his Son from heaven – Jesus, whom he raised from the dead, and who rescues us from the coming wrath'.

What Paul says about the gospel in 1 Thessalonians 1:10 is brief – he refers to the resurrection and to Christians' future salvation from wrath, but says nothing about the manner of Christ's death or what that meant. That is because the Thessalonians were clearly concerned about whether or not they would come under divine wrath. So at the very beginning of his letter, Paul reminds them of the implications of their faith; since God has raised Jesus from the dead, they can be sure of their own future salvation. In 5:10, he assures them again that they will be saved from wrath 'through our Lord Jesus Christ',

> who died for us
> in order that (whether we are awake or asleep) we may live with him.

The clause that I have put in brackets has been included by Paul because the Thessalonians have been disturbed by the death of some of their number, and he is anxious to assure them that these people will nevertheless be included in the coming salvation from wrath. Without it, we have a two-line couplet:

> who died for us
> in order that we may live with him.

Paul's stark comment that Christ died 'for us' is balanced by an assurance that we will share his resurrection. Remarkably, however, though Christ's resurrection is clearly implied in the 'with him', we have no 'who rose' to match the 'who died'; instead, we have a purpose clause, introduced by the Greek word *hina,* meaning 'in order that'. We shall discover that Paul is fond of this particular construction.

'Christ died *for us*'. What does Paul mean by this? Some commentators assume that Paul is thinking of Christ's death as substitutionary: they assume, that is, that Christ dies *in our place.*[1] This does not seem to be an appropriate description of his teaching, however, for Christ's death does not mean that Christians do not face physical death.[2] It is possible that the Thessalonians had assumed that this was the case, and that this is why they were disturbed by the fact that some of their number had already died (1 Thess. 4:13). If so, they had misunderstood Paul's gospel: Christ's death does not put a stop to physical death *in this age*. Christians may be 'awake or asleep' – alive or dead – when, as Paul expected would happen soon, the Day of Judgement came.

Had Paul been thinking of Christ's death as substitutionary, he would have written simply 'Christ died for us, in order that we might live'. In physical terms, such substitutions are possible. A famous, fictional, example occurs at the end of Dickens' novel, *A Tale of Two Cities,* when Sydney Carton takes Charles Darnay's place at the guillotine. But such events are not always fictions. A friend of mine dived under a Calcutta tram to save a child who had fallen beneath it, and died as a result. Her death could truly be described as substitutionary, since she died in order that the child might live.

Christ our representative

Paul, however, is using a different concept: 'Christ died', he wrote, 'in order that we might live *with him.*' He sees Christians as *sharing* the life of Christ. This is the idea that we find him spelling out in Romans 6: 'Christ died for us' does not mean that we escape death, but that he dies as our representative – the representative of humanity – and those who in turn share his death (to sin) will also share his resurrection. Living with Christ, therefore, implies also *dying* with him.

A similar idea is expressed in another of Paul's early letters – this time in very personal terms. In Galatians 2:19–21, Paul exclaims, 'I have died to law, *in order that* I might live to God.' How has this death taken place? It was by being 'crucified with Christ', so that it is now *Christ* who lives in Paul. Once again, Christ's resurrection is implied, not spelt out. This new life derives from the fact that the Son of God 'loved me and gave himself *for me*'. Reverse the order of the sentences, and we see the parallel with 1 Thessalonians 5:10:

> The Son of God loved me and gave himself for me,
> (and I have died to the law)
> in order that I might live to God;
> (I have been crucified with Christ)
> and it is no longer I who live,
> but Christ who lives in me.

Galatians 2 fills out what is said in 1 Thessalonians 5:10, reminding us that Christ's death on behalf of others has to be appropriated: it is those who share his death to life in the old age who will share his resurrection life.

In other summaries, Christ's death is linked specifically with sins. In Galatians 1:4, the Galatians are reminded that

> Christ gave himself *for our sins,*
> that he might set us free from this present evil age.

We have seen already that 'this age' is dominated by the power of sin.[3]

In 1 Corinthians 15:3, we are again told that 'Christ died *for our sins*', but this time, Paul notes that this was 'according to the scriptures'. Unfortunately he does not tell us *which* scriptures! One possibility is that he was thinking of Isaiah 53, a passage which came to be interpreted of Christ. It is unclear whether or not it was understood in this way in Paul's day, though it certainly was by the time that 1 Peter 2:21–5 was written. Nor is it clear whether he is linking the phrase with the fact of Christ's death or with its purpose, to deal with sin. Perhaps, like the phrase 'witnessed to by the law and the prophets' in Romans 3:21, it is meant to refer to the scriptures in general.

Another passage which links Christ's death with sins – or rather with trespasses (the term he uses in Romans 5) – is Romans 4:25, which refers to those who believe in Jesus our Lord,

> who was handed over to death because of *our trespasses,*
> and was raised because of *our acquittal* (or 'so that we might be declared righteous').

This time, we have two parallel statements about Christ's death and resurrection: his death was the result of our trespasses, and his resurrection led to our acquittal. If we try to unpack their meaning, however, we realize that this is based on an understanding of Christ's resurrection similar to that which we find in 1 Thessalonians 5:10:

> He was handed over to death (because of our trespasses)
> and was raised in order that we might share his acquittal (pronounced at his resurrection).

As we have seen, this is the idea that Paul then spells out in Romans 5, in his comparison and contrast between Adam and Christ.

The same ideas reappear in 2 Corinthians 5:14–15, where Paul writes 'One has died for all'. Once again, this sounds at first like substitution, Christ dying *instead of* all, but as we read on, we find that he explains that what he means is that Christ died *as our representative*. He immediately spells out the significance of this 'death for all':

> One has died *for all*,
> therefore *all have died*.
> And he died *for all*
> *in order that* the living might no longer live to themselves,
> but to the one who died and was raised for them.

This time, therefore, Paul has explained what he means when he says that Christ died 'for all'. It means that they, too, have already died – not, of course, a physical death, but a spiritual one, to sin. As usual, the consequence is life – described here not, as in 1 Thessalonians, as life with Christ, but life that is centred on him, instead of on themselves. This is parallel to what he says in Galatians 2:20, where he speaks of his new life as a life centred on the Son of God.

Sharing in Christ's righteousness

It is hardly surprising that Paul goes on, in 2 Corinthians 5:17, to explain that when someone is 'in Christ', there is in effect 'a new creation'. The old things (life lived as Adam lived it, dominated by sin and condemnation) have gone, and new things (life in Christ, and the righteousness that is found in him) have arrived. This is the fulfilment of the eschatological promise – a restoration which is in fact a new beginning.

All this, Paul explains, is from God, who has initiated the whole process of reconciliation. He did this in Christ. How? Paul explains in 5:21:

> The one who knew no sin
> He made to be sin *for us*,
> *in order that* we might become the righteousness of God *in him*.

Once again we have the familiar 'for us' and 'in order that', but the idea itself is new and shocking. Instead of Christ *dying* for us, we have him being *made sin.* What does Paul mean? We should note that he does *not* say that Christ was made a *sinner:* indeed, he specifically notes that he 'knew no sin'. The idea that he was 'made sin' is in fact close to one that we have met before, in Romans 5:12–21 and 8:3. As man, 'in Adam', Christ was identified with the human predicament and shared the consequences of sin – estrangement from God. That he was 'made sin' was demonstrated in his death, just as his resurrection demonstrated his righteousness. But Paul makes no specific reference to either his death or his resurrection. Instead, he points to the *cause* of his death – human sin – and the *result* of his resurrection – our righteousness. If Christ was 'made sin', Christians 'become righteousness', and just as being made sin signified alienation from God, so being made righteousness signifies reconciliation. But once again, it depends on that significant phrase 'in him'. Christians share in *Christ's* righteousness. For all Paul's startling language, we recognize the similarities with what he says in Romans 4:25:

> He was handed over to death because of our trespasses,
> And was raised that we might be declared righteous.

His death was a judgement on our sin – a judgement whose consequences he shared. His resurrection was a vindication of his righteousness – a vindication in whose consequences *we* share.

From 2 Corinthians we turn back to 1 Corinthians, where we find an 'echo' of 2 Corinthians 5:21. We have noted already Paul's insistence on the importance of the message of Christ crucified (1:18–21). It is in the context of this passage that he describes what it means to be 'in Christ Jesus', who is for believers not only wisdom from God, but *righteousness* and sanctification and redemption as well (v. 30). Paul's discussion of the message of the cross here has underlined its absurdity: the cross seems to be a symbol of weakness and folly. Its true meaning is now experienced by those who are united with Christ: believers share Christ's righteousness.

It seems clear that Paul's understanding of how the death of Christ can lead to forgiveness and to righteousness depends on two central factors. Firstly, whatever happened was the work of God himself, who 'sent' his Son, 'gave him up', and 'raised' him from the dead. Secondly, it was achieved *through* Christ, who (as Son of God) was obedient to his will, but was also *fully human*. In order to be our representative, he had to be one with us, sharing in what it meant to be human. As we noted in looking at Romans 5, what he achieved was as 'the one man, Jesus Christ'.

In Galatians 3:13 we find Paul using language quite as shocking as that which he uses in 2 Corinthians 5:21. This time he describes Christ as 'a curse'. In this passage, he links the curse pronounced by the law on those who fail to obey it (Deut. 27:26) with its declaration that a criminal whose body was hung on a tree was under a curse (Deut. 21:23).

Such a person himself became a curse – a source of contamination to others. Christ's death was the proclamation that, under the law, he was a curse; in fact he had become a source of blessing, and had 'redeemed' (set free) those who were under that curse. Once again, Paul links what happened to Christ and what happens to believers with the Greek word *hina*, meaning 'in order that':

> Christ redeemed us from the curse of the law,
> having become a curse *for us* . . .
> *in order that* the blessing of Abraham might be extended, *in Christ*, to the Gentiles,
> (and) *in order that* we might receive the promised Spirit through faith.

Paul's argument here is specifically related to the role of the law, and to his fear lest the Galatian Christians should see it as necessary to salvation. Instead of speaking of sin and righteousness as in 2 Corinthians 5, therefore, he focuses on the more specific issues relating to the law, which had pronounced a curse on sinners, but had not led to the blessing promised to Abraham. As a Jew, crucified by Rome, Christ had come under this curse, but the curse had been overturned; Jews and Gentiles alike had received blessing, and proof of this was to be seen in the gift of the Holy Spirit. Once again, as in 1 Thessalonians 5:10, there is no specific reference to Christ's resurrection, but it is the underlying assumption of his argument: there could be no blessing without it. Just as what appeared to human eyes (which see things from the point of view of the 'flesh') to be folly and weakness proved to be wisdom and strength (1 Cor. 1:25), so what seemed in the eyes of the law (which operated in the sphere of the 'flesh') to be a curse has now been demonstrated to be the true source of blessing.

We have suggested that Paul's understanding of Christ as having become a curse, set out in Galatians 3, is linked with the fact that he was a Jew. This is an idea which Paul spells out in the following chapter, when he says that God's Son was 'born of a woman, born under the law'. If we read on, we discover that what Paul says here has the familiar structure, using the Greek word *hina,* meaning 'in order that', that we have seen in statements about Christ's death:

> God sent his Son,
>   Born of a woman,
> Born under the law,
> *in order that* he might redeem those under the law,
> *in order that* we might receive adoption.

The structure is similar to that in Galatians 3:13–14, but so, too, are the ideas. What Christ did in being identified with the human (and specifically Jewish) situation was done *in order that* human beings might enjoy certain blessings. In 3:13–14, as a result of being redeemed from the curse of the law, Christians have received the promised blessing of the Spirit, and Gentiles have been included in the blessing promised to Abraham (namely, righteousness). In 4:4–5, too, Paul speaks of the redemption of those who are under the law, and of the gift of sonship – a gift that he has already said is given to those who are 'in' Christ, and so the offspring of Abraham (3:26, 29), and which is guaranteed by the gift of the Spirit (4:6).

If Galatians 3 and 4 offer parallel ideas, so do Galatians 4 and Romans 8. In Romans 8:3, as in Galatians 4:4, we read once more that God sent his Son – this time in the likeness of sinful flesh. Once again, we find Paul insisting that Christ shared fully in our humanity. Moreover, God condemned sin in the flesh (a condemnation that, as he has already explained, led to Christ's death). The purpose this time (introduced once again by *hina*) is said to be that the law's requirement of righteousness should be fulfilled in us, who live according to the Spirit (Rom. 8:4) – the Spirit of holiness who raised Christ (and us) from the dead (Rom. 1:4); when that takes place, we receive the 'Spirit of adoption' (8:15), and so address God as 'Father', as in Galatians 4:6.

Here then, we have two statements that God sent his Son to share our humanity, in order that those who are 'in him' might share his status as God's children. Paul uses the same idea elsewhere. A notable example is in Philippians, where Paul describes Jesus as being 'in the form of God', and yet taking 'the form of a slave' by taking human likeness. There could be no greater contrast than this – especially since his action led to death on a cross (Phil. 2:6–11). This passage spells out more clearly than any other what sharing the status of men and women really involved. But Paul does not explain that what Christ did was 'for us', and neither is there a *hina* clause to explain what his self-humiliation achieved – only a triumphant 'Therefore' in verse 9 which introduces an account of how God has exalted him. This time Paul seems to tell us how Christ became man, and to describe his death and resurrection (or rather, appropriately here, his *exaltation,* since Paul has been stressing Christ's great humiliation) *without* telling us what these achieve for others. But when we turn the page and read the end of chapter 3, we find that Paul here describes how believers confidently hope to *share Christ's status*. Because he experienced human humiliation and death, he will enable believers to share his glory: once again then, the fact that Christ shared our status means that we shall share his. If the emphasis in this letter is rather different from that in Romans and Galatians, being concerned with future hope rather than present experience, that is hardly surprising, since when Paul wrote Philippians, he was writing from prison, facing the prospect of an imminent death-sentence. What he had in mind here was the end of the process, as described in Romans 8, when those who are already acknowledged as God's children would be conformed to the glory of his Son.

We find a similar idea, expressed in very different language, in 2 Corinthians 8:9. Here, thrown into a discussion of what we might have supposed was a very mundane subject (the need for the Corinthians to contribute to the collection that Paul is making for the benefit of poor Christians in Jerusalem!) Paul tosses a reminder of what Christ has done for *them:*

> You know the grace of our Lord Jesus Christ:
> that, though he was rich, yet on your account he became poor,
> *in order that* you, by his poverty, might become rich.

The implication is obvious: if Christ did so much for you, you certainly should help those who are poorer than yourselves. Here we see Paul adapting a central theme of his understanding of what Christ has done 'for us', and expressing it in language which will be appropriate to a particular application of its implications. Instead of speaking of Christ being born of a woman, under law, coming in the likeness of sinful flesh, or coming in the form of a slave, he describes him as accepting 'poverty' instead of riches. But here, again, we find the idea that Christians share *his* status. Because he became poor, they become rich. The language is, of course, metaphorical. But it nevertheless provides a theological basis for Paul's appeal.

With the exception of Philippians 2 and 3, these statements are parallel in structure with other statements that we have looked at which spell out the purpose of what Christ did in the form of clear contrasts. These were:

- 1 Thess. 5:10, where the result of Christ's death for us was that we live with him;
- Gal. 3:13–14, where Christ became a curse for us, and the result was blessing (sonship and Spirit) for Gentiles as well as for Jews; and
- 2 Cor. 5:21, where Christ became sin, with the result that we became righteousness in him.

We see, then, that whether Paul is talking about what theologians later came to speak of as the doctrine of 'incarnation',[4] or about what they termed the doctrine of 'atonement', he uses similar formulae. Because he was fully human, Christ *shared the status* of men and women, and shared in what it meant to be human; this involved suffering the consequences of sin, including death. In raising him from the dead, God has declared him to be righteous, given him life, and initiated a new creation, and those who are in Christ *share his status*. It is because they are 'in Christ' and share his status that they have been 'righted'. It is this idea of sharing in Christ's status which a nineteenth-century hymn-writer, William Bright, was attempting to express when he prayed that God would 'only look on us as found in him'.[5] An early father of the church, Irenaeus, summed up the concept of mutual sharing of status even more memorably when he wrote: 'Christ became what we are, in order that we might become what he himself is'.[6] He became what we are – and shared in all that this means – so that we might share in what *he* is.

'Interchange in Christ'

This idea of mutual sharing seems to lie at the heart of Paul's understanding of how the human race has been reconciled to

God. In trying to describe what takes place, I have adopted the term 'interchange' – a word that I have used in an attempt to convey the mutuality of experience involved.[7] It should be noted that it is *not* an 'exchange' between Christ and the believer. An exchange would imply substitution, of the kind illustrated in Charles Dickens' story.[8] What Paul is describing is God's Son sharing fully in our humanity, and suffering the consequences of so doing, so that he shares our human death. Yet he refused to succumb to sin (2 Cor. 5:21) and was obedient to God (Rom. 5:19). Therefore God raised him from death, and vindicated him. Because he shared our humanity, he is able to act as our representative. He died to sin on our behalf, and has been raised to a life in which we, too, may share. But in order to share this new life, Paul insists that believers have to be baptized into Christ – and so, symbolically, into his death – acknowledging God's judgement on sin. Thus Christ *shares* our physical death and we *share* his death to sin and his life. This is no simple exchange! But for believers, there is certainly *an exchange of experience:* instead of sin, they have righteousness, instead of slavery, freedom, instead of death, life – and all because they now share the status of the Son of God, and acknowledge God himself as 'Father'.

From time to time, Paul uses various images to convey what Christ's death achieves. In Galatians 3:13 and 4:5, as we have seen, he uses a word which means 'to redeem' or 'to buy back' – the word used in 'redeeming' a slave – and in 1 Corinthians 6:20 and 7:23 he uses the simple verb 'to buy' in order to remind the Corinthians that they belong to God (cf. the similar argument in Rom. 6:15–23). Earlier, in 1 Corinthians 5:7, he refers to Christ as the passover lamb, sacrificed for us, a reminder that the blood of the passover lamb played a crucial part in God's rescue of Israel from Egypt, and became a symbol for God's redemption of his people. And we have seen how, in Romans, Paul made use of two other Old Testament images, with what appears to be an allusion to the mercy-seat in 3:23, and a possible reference to the sin-offering in Romans 8:3.

There is nothing surprising in Paul's use of these images. He has maintained that what the law and the prophets promised had been fulfilled in Christ, and there seems no reason to suppose that Paul is using ideas that he has 'borrowed' from others, or which do not fit with his own understanding of what the death of Jesus achieved. Sin had to be dealt with, and sacrificial imagery was appropriate to explain what had been done. When the original passover lambs were killed, the result was freedom for Israel; the sacrifice of a sin-offering had symbolized the removal of sins; the 'mercy-seat' was the place where God and his people were reconciled, through the death of an animal. But it was no longer an animal that had been sacrificed; instead it was the 'one man' who was able to bring God and man together whose death had finally dealt with sin.

What we have discovered, in looking at Paul's teaching about how Christ's death affects the human race, is firstly, that he insists that the initiative is with God. It is *God* who reconciles (2 Cor. 5:18–20; Rom. 5:10–11), *God* who sends his Son (Rom. 8:3; Gal. 4:4), *God* who gives him up (Rom. 4:25; 8:32), *God* whose grace is seen in what Christ does for us (Rom. 5:15–17). Secondly, we have seen that Christ shares fully in our status, and that as a result, Christ dies *for us,* not as our substitute but as our representative. Thirdly, we have seen that he is our representative not only in his death but in his resurrection also: because he has shared our status, we are enabled to share his. What Paul understands this interchange of experience to mean for the life of a Christian is the topic that we must explore next.

10
Life 'in Christ'

'Christ became what we are, in order that we might become what he is.' What, then, does it mean for the believer to become what Christ is – to become 'like' him?

We have rejected the view that interprets Paul's understanding of Christ's death as substitutionary. In Paul's teaching, Christ dies as our representative, not as our substitute: since Christ's death was a death to sin, Christians must share that death. That means that when believers accept as their own Christ's death to sinful existence, they have taken the first step to sharing in what Christ now is. It is necessary, then, for Christians to share Christ's death, before they can share his resurrection.

This sharing in Christ's death and resurrection were aptly symbolized for Paul by baptism, since this served as a dramatic representation of what was taking place in the believer's life. In baptism, the convert was 'buried' beneath the waters and emerged from them again, so symbolizing death to sin and resurrection to a new life. Baptism was a once-in-a-lifetime event, but as a symbolic action, it pointed to the reality it signified – a reality that was worked out in various ways, in the past, in the present and in the future.

Christ *had* died and he *had* been raised, and in a sense the Christian *had* died to sin with Christ and *had* been raised to a new life of righteousness. That much lay in the past. But dying to sin and living to righteousness still needed to be worked out continually in the life of the believer, as we saw when looking at Romans 6. They were an on-going process.

This process is not simply negative – about dying to sin – but positive. It is about sharing Christ's life – about becoming like him. We have seen already how Paul talks about Christians being conformed to Christ's image (Rom. 8:29; 2 Cor. 3:18), and sharing his status as God's 'sons' (Rom. 8:14; Gal. 4:6–7). But what does it mean to become like him? What was the earthly Jesus like? Because Paul tells us little about Jesus' life, he says little about his character, except in very broad terms. In Romans 15:1, he declares that 'those of us who are strong should bear the weaknesses of those who are weak and not please ourselves . . . For Christ did not please himself', as scripture demonstrates. If Paul refers to scripture rather than tradition about Jesus' sufferings, that may have been because he regarded it as more authoritative: Christians must heed what it says (v. 4). In 15:7, he urges the Romans to 'welcome one another . . . as Christ welcomed' them, but it was clearly the exalted Christ, not the earthly Jesus, who had welcomed gentile Christians. Nevertheless he goes on to remind them that it was by becoming 'a servant to the circumcised' that he was able 'to confirm the promises made to the patriarchs' and so enable 'the Gentiles to glorify God' (vv. 8–9). Christ's service to the circumcised, then, is not only the foundation of their present existence, but also the pattern which they must emulate.

Elsewhere, we find occasional references to Christ's love for us (Rom. 8:35; 2 Cor. 5:14; Gal. 2:20) and to his obedience (Rom. 5:19; Phil. 2:8). His love is something that the Christian is expected to share; if it is no longer Paul who lives but Christ who lives in him, then it must be the love of Christ – the love that led Christ to give himself up for Paul's sake – that motivates Paul (Gal. 2:20) – as 2 Corinthians 5:14 also states. If Adam's disobedience was shared by the whole human race, then clearly those who now live in Adam rather than in Christ must share his obedience (Rom. 5:19). In Philippians, Paul follows what is said about Jesus' obedience in 2:6–11 with a 'therefore' in v. 12: therefore, those who share the mind of Christ (2:5) must obey, since God himself is at work in them. Once again, what Christ did is both the foundation of Christian life and its pattern.

The faithfulness of Christ

Paul links both the love of Christians and their obedience with the love and obedience of Christ. What about faith? 'Faith' is the English translation usually adopted for rendering the Greek word *pistis,* which can, however, be translated in a variety of ways. *Pistis* can mean 'faith' or 'trust', but it can mean, too, the 'faithfulness' which is the basis of others' trust; it can also mean the 'belief' held by those who have faith. When used as an attribute of God, the word refers to his faithfulness (Rom. 3:3); when used of men and women, it normally means 'trust', reliance on someone, but can again mean 'faithfulness' (Gal. 5:22). Like *pistis,* the English word 'faith' is itself ambiguous, since it can be used not only of trust but also of *the* faith, meaning a particular set of beliefs.

Would we expect Paul to think of Christ himself as being faithful to God's will and trusting in him? The answer is obviously 'Yes', since obedience to God that is motivated by love must be based on trust. As we have seen, righteousness is bestowed on those who have faith – who trust in God – but this righteousness is not *their own* righteousness but the righteousness *of Christ,* which they share because they are in him. Christ is *the* righteous one, and if the righteous live by faith, as Habakkuk and Paul both affirm (Hab. 2:4; Rom. 1:17; Gal. 3:11), then presumably Christ himself had faith – or trust – in God. Does Paul specifically say so? There are, in fact, several places where Paul speaks of 'the faith of Christ', but because of the ambiguity of the Greek construction, this phrase can mean either 'faith *in* Christ' or 'the faith *of* Christ'. If Paul was thinking of 'the faith *of* Christ', then he could be referring either to his faithfulness or to his trust in God (Rom. 3:22, 26; Gal. 2:16 (twice), 20; 3:22;[1] Phil. 3:9). Until recently, all translators assumed that Paul was talking about faith *in* Christ, but it is arguable that it was the Reformation emphasis on the doctrine of 'justification by faith' which led them to do so.[2] That does not mean, however, that translating the phrase as 'the faith of Christ' is inconsistent with that doctrine. It is perhaps significant that Paul uses the phrase *only* in contexts where he is clearly describing how believers are righted by trusting in what God has done in Christ – i.e. where he is writing about 'justification by faith'. If Paul is using the phrase in the sense of 'faith in Christ', then he is merely emphasizing the point. If he is referring to Christ's own faith (or faithfulness) then he is grounding the faith of believers in that of Christ himself.

There is, indeed, much to be said, grammatically and exegetically, for understanding the phrase to refer primarily to Christ's own faithfulness or to his trust in God.[3] It is because Christ trusted in God that there is righteousness for all who believe (Rom. 3:22). It is because of his faithfulness or trust that Christians are righted, for 'we have trusted in him, so that we might be righted through his faithfulness' (Gal. 2:16). Paul has no righteousness of his own; what he does have, in Christ, is the righteousness that comes through the faith (or faithfulness) of Christ, and which is based on faith (Phil. 3:9). If this is Paul's meaning, then we share the love, obedience and trust that led Christ to the cross, as well as his righteousness. Because believers are 'in Christ', the 'faith of Christ' – his faithfulness and trust in God – is shared by them and undergirds their faith or trust in him.[4]

By baptism, Christians share not only in Christ's death to sin, but in his resurrection life also. Since his resurrection vindicated what he was, and gave the seal of approval to his love, to his obedience, to his faithfulness and his trust in God, that must mean that Christians who share in that resurrection life are expected to share these attitudes. The reality symbolized by baptism – dying and rising with Christ – is worked out in the present lives of Christians when they cease to demand their own rights and adopt the attitudes that led Christ to the cross. Writing to the Philippians, Paul urges them to live in accordance with the mind that they see in Christ and that belongs – or should belong! – to those who are 'in' Christ. That means sharing the mind of one who gave up everything and was obedient to death, even the most humiliating and gruesome of deaths on a cross (Phil. 2:5–8).

Conformity to Christ

There has been much discussion about the precise meaning of Paul's command in Philippians 2:5. Does he mean 'Have the mind which *was* in Christ Jesus', and which is demonstrated in his self-emptying and obedience to death? Or does he mean 'Have the mind which you already share as those who are *in* Christ Jesus'? In fact, the contrast is a false one. It is clear that Paul is appealing to the way in which Jesus himself behaved: he is their 'example'. But it is clear also that he is appealing to them as a community of believers 'in Christ' (Phil. 2:1) to show the attitudes appropriate to those who belong to him. His appeal is not simply to 'imitate' Christ, but to be conformed to what he is *because* they are already 'in him'. It was only because 'he emptied himself . . . and humbled himself . . . and was obedient to death' that the Philippian Christians are in Christ at all. It is impossible, then, for them to live 'in Christ' without sharing the mind – the attitudes – of Jesus. Impossible, that is, unless they deny the gospel itself, the whole rationale of their life as Christians.[5]

Paul's understanding of the Christian life is, then, that it means being conformed to Christ's likeness. At its simplest, it can be described as allowing Christ to live *in* one. In Galatians 2:19–20 he writes: 'I have been crucified with Christ. It is no longer I who live but Christ who lives in me.' That means that those who come into contact with Paul should see and experience what Christ himself is like. It is a bold claim!

Turning back to the previous chapter of Galatians, we find Paul describing his conversion/call (Gal. 1:15–16). As we have already seen, his account of this is very brief: 'When it pleased God, who set me apart from my mother's womb and called me by his grace, to reveal his Son in me – in order that I might take the good news about him to the Gentiles . . .' Although translations generally assume that Paul means that 'it pleased God . . . to reveal his Son *to*' him, his use of the Greek preposition *en,* meaning 'in', is surely significant. He is not talking simply about the time when God revealed the identity of his Son *to* him, but of his call to proclaim God's Son to the Gentiles. And he was to do this, not by word of mouth alone, but by allowing Christ to live *in* him. God revealed his Son to the Gentiles *in* Paul, in his manner of life, as well as in his preaching. Hence Paul's appeals to his converts to remember how he himself had behaved while among them, and his demands that they 'imitate' him. We tend to regard this as a sign of pride and self-satisfaction on his part, but Paul is simply taking his apostolic calling seriously. Christians are called on to imitate Christ. How are they to know what Christ is like? By listening to the gospel and by looking at those *in whose lives* God is revealing his Son, because he lives *in* them. In demanding that his converts imitate him, then, Paul is asking them, not to look at *himself* but at Christ, who is *in* him.

Paul's claim, then, is that the crucifixion and resurrection of Christ are stamped on his life. This means sharing in the 'mind' of Christ – the mind that led him to the cross. It means sharing in his death to sin, in his resurrection to life in the Spirit, and in his righteousness – his 'rightness' in relation to God. In this sharing, however, Paul is not unique! As an apostle, sent to the Gentiles, he is God's instrument to reveal God's Son to them. Just as he imitates Christ, so they, in turn, must imitate him (1 Cor. 11:1).

But what did that mean in practice? This appeal to the Corinthians comes at the end of a lengthy discussion (which we will look at again in our next chapter) about how to behave in connection with a particular ethical problem that was troubling the Corinthian church. As we shall see, Paul's response to this question focuses on the issue of love for others. Christ died for their weaker brothers (1 Cor. 8:11); therefore they must be concerned for their welfare. Paul himself has given up many things for the sake of winning converts to the gospel (1 Corinthians 9). In a striking echo of what he says elsewhere about Christ sharing our human situation – taking the form of a slave (Phil. 2:7), being born under the law (Gal. 4:4), becoming sin, though himself without sin (2 Cor. 5:21) – he describes how he has made himself a slave to all, and has been 'as under the law for those under the law' (though not himself under the law), 'outside the law for those outside the law', *in order that* he might win them for the gospel (1 Cor. 9:19–23). This was no idle boast. His mission to Gentiles had indeed put him 'outside the law' in the eyes of many strict Jews, since he had eaten with Gentiles (Gal. 2:11–14). Writing to the Galatians, he points out that he has become as they are (i.e. 'outside the law'), and so appeals to them to become as he is (4:12), 'set free from the law' (4:5).

Paul sees himself, then, as sharing in the work of the gospel, and being 'conformed' to the pattern of 'interchange' that he sees in Christ. Just as the Son of God identified himself with the human condition in order that those to whom he had been sent might be saved, so Paul, sent to proclaim the gospel to the Gentiles, has made himself 'outside the law' for their sake.[6] Paul understands his call to be not simply to *preach* the gospel, but to *perform* it.

Summing up his argument at the end of 1 Corinthians 10, Paul urges the Corinthians to consider, in all their actions, the interests of everyone, whether Jews or Greeks – just as he himself strives to do (vv. 32–3). This is why they must imitate him, just as he imitates Christ (11:1).

Paul as role model

Earlier in the same epistle, Paul had already appealed to the Corinthians to imitate him (4:16). This appeal, too, is made in the context of a discussion about Paul's role as an apostle, and comes towards the end of a lengthy justification of Paul's manner of life. It seems clear that the Corinthians expected their leaders to be men of whom they could be proud – men who were recognized for their wisdom and fluency of speech, who were suitably rewarded by being accorded status in the community, and who therefore enjoyed honour and riches. Moreover, they assumed that any reputable teacher would offer *them* similar benefits: they assumed that Paul's 'good news' would bring *them* esoteric wisdom, status and power.

Paul apparently felt that he had cut a sorry figure among the Corinthians: 'I came to you in weakness and in fear and in much trembling', he wrote, 'and my speech and my preaching were not in plausible words of wisdom.' Nevertheless, the Spirit had worked through him, and the power of God had led them to believe (2:3–5). His way of preaching the gospel had thus been a *demonstration* of the gospel, which was about the power of God working through weakness, and the wisdom of God being found in something that appeared to be utterly foolish – in other words, it had embodied the message of Christ crucified. Power through weakness was the message of the gospel, and it was the mode of Paul's proclamation of it also (1:18–31).

Although they had responded to Paul's preaching, some of the Corinthians were clearly uneasy with the way that he saw his role. For the pattern of the gospel – power through weakness, wisdom through folly – was stamped not only on the way in which he delivered his message, but on his whole manner of life as well. Although Paul was insistent that he was an apostle (1 Cor. 1:1; 9:1), he was clear that his calling was to serve Christ, and not to demand honour for himself. The Corinthians must think of the apostles 'as servants of Christ[7] and stewards of God's mysteries' he tells them (4:1). Paul had carried out the particular task assigned to him, much as would a gardener tending the plants in his care (3:5–9). In a sarcastic outburst he contrasts the way in which the Corinthian Christians see themselves – able to do anything, possessing riches, reigning like kings (4:8) – with the reality of his own everyday life.

Paul's language echoes some of the claims made by the Stoics, and it seems that the Corinthians may have been making similar claims to theirs, seeing their faith as a rival philosophy that gives them superior status because of their superior knowledge. They considered themselves to be 'wise in Christ' and 'strong', and expected to be treated with 'honour' (v. 10). They had clearly seized on the joys promised by the gospel, and assumed that they could all be experienced here and now. They had embraced the idea of 'living with Christ', but had forgotten that 'dying with Christ' also needed to be worked out in their present way of life, and that they were called to share Christ's shame and lack of status. In other words, they were behaving as though the End had already come, and were claiming to be enjoying already things that belonged to the future, resurrection life.

Paul, meanwhile, was experiencing what it meant to be conformed to Christ's image and to live out the gospel. It meant being 'hungry and thirsty', being 'poorly clothed and beaten up and of no fixed abode' (v. 11). No wonder Paul said that he was treated as a fool, and had to endure weakness and disgrace (v. 10). He grew weary, working with his hands (v. 12) – 'the more fool you!' we can imagine some of the Corinthians saying. Why not enjoy the hospitality that he might expect, as a respected teacher? Paul has been reviled, persecuted and slandered, and in response he has praised others, endured suffering and tried to be conciliatory. He has been treated like refuse, like the scum of society (4:12–13). Later in the epistle he will explain that he has deliberately put up with the toil involved in supporting himself, lest he put any hindrance in the way of the gospel (9:12). It demonstrates his determination to make himself a slave to others, in order to win them for the gospel (9:19).

The Corinthians would expect to model themselves on their leaders. It is clear why they would not be eager to model themselves on Paul – and were thus in danger of renouncing his gospel. Yet Paul now appeals to them, as their 'father' in the gospel, to imitate him (4:15–16). As their father, Paul expects them to follow his example, and he has therefore sent Timothy to remind them of Paul's 'way of life in Christ' – something that he teaches in *all* the churches.

Paul reminds the Corinthians of his insistence on working to support himself in 1 Corinthians 4:12 and 9:1–18, in order to demonstrate how he lives out the gospel, and on both occasions he follows this reminder with an appeal to imitate his example (4:16; 11:1). This topic is the subject of a similar appeal to the Thessalonians, in 2 Thessalonians. Although the authorship of this letter is questioned by some scholars it may well be authentic, and certainly the remarks on this matter sound genuine (3:6–13). Paul reminds the Thessalonians that they 'know how you should imitate us, for we were not idle when we were among you, and we did not eat bread belonging to anyone without paying for it, but worked night and day, in toil and drudgery, in order not to be a burden to any of you'. The letter, written in the names of Paul, Silvanus and Timothy, presumably includes all three in the 'we'. Otherwise Paul would hardly have persuaded the Thessalonians that they must do the same, which was apparently his intention: Paul and his co-workers did it, we are told, in order to provide the Thessalonians with an example to imitate (3:7–9).

The Thessalonians had, in fact, already followed the example of others, and been commended for doing so. In 1 Thessalonians, also written in the names of Paul, Silvanus and Timothy, they are reminded of the way in which they responded to the gospel – *not simply in word* but in power, since they knew 'what we were like for your sakes': once again, Paul and his companions had clearly endeavoured to live the gospel, and not just to preach it (1:5). As a result, the Thessalonians 'became imitators, both of us and of the Lord', and then, in turn, became themselves 'an example to all the believers in Macedonia and in Achaia (1:6–7). What Paul understands this imitation to involve we see a little later in the epistle, when he prays that the Lord will make their love for one another increase and overflow, just as his does for them (3:12). The key principle is love, of which concern for one another, demonstrated in Paul's refusal to expect others to support him, is a part.

Turning back to the letter to the Philippians, we realize how this theme of 'imitation' of the apostle is rooted in the concept of 'conformity' to the likeness of Christ. We have seen how, in 2:5–11, the Philippians are urged to have the mind of Christ: they are to be of one mind, to share a common love, to be in agreement, think alike, to do nothing from selfish ambition or conceit, but humbly regard others as better than themselves; they are to be concerned for others' interests rather than their own (2:2–4).

In Philippians 3, Paul describes something of his own experience, telling how he abandoned his Jewish privileges in order to be found in Christ. Interestingly, his account mirrors the story he tells about Christ, for Paul too, had turned his back on the privileges that were his birthright and had been rewarded with something even better (3:4–11). Because Christ gave up what he had, and experienced humiliation and death, he was 'highly exalted' and confessed as Lord. Paul gave up his Jewish privileges, including his righteousness in the eyes of the law, 'in order to gain Christ and to be found in him' and to share *his* righteousness, which is a righteousness bestowed by God (vv. 9–10). Paul's call/conversion meant a willingness to be conformed to the pattern that he sees in Christ, which begins with the abandonment of status, with humiliation and death. Paul's aim was to know 'the power of Christ's resurrection' – clearly already at work in his life – and 'the fellowship of his sufferings', which are also part of his present experience (v. 10). Still to come is the expectation that he will become 'like him in his death' and that he will 'attain the resurrection of the dead'. Thus Paul, facing the possibility of imminent death, trusts that he will experience what it means to die and rise with Christ in the future.

Paul's story relates his particular way – as a Jew – of being shaped by the gospel story. But he expects others, too, to reflect that story in their lives. We have seen how the gospel-summary in Philippians 2:6–11 is set in a context of exhortation that can be summed up in words such as 'Be like this; behave like this'. Now, at the end of Philippians 3, Paul refers sadly to those who live as 'enemies of the cross of Christ', denying the relevance of the story for their lives by pursuing physical pleasures and boasting about things which should have made them ashamed (3:18–19). In contrast to them, however, there are those who live according to the example being given by Paul and those who try to live as those who 'know Christ' (vv. 17, 10). Paul summons the Philippians, perhaps to join in imitating him or perhaps to be joint-imitators *with* him, i.e. of Christ (the Greek is ambiguous). Whichever it is, the ultimate 'example' is Christ himself, though he is far *more* than an example, since it is 'the power of his resurrection' that is being worked out in their lives, as they share his resurrection life. But there is more to come, since they are awaiting the coming of their Saviour who, by the power that enables him to subject everything to himself, will change the likeness of their bodies of humiliation, conforming them to his own glorious body (v. 21).

The language of this passage echoes that of 2:6–11, reminding us once again that Paul believed that Christ became what we are (accepting the form of a slave and the likeness of a man) and humbled himself, but has now been exalted above all things. If we share his humiliation, argues Paul, we shall share his glory also – a view that he repeats in Romans 8, when reminding his readers that the promise that Christians will inherit what God has in store for them depends on their willingness to embrace suffering. We will share in Christ's inheritance, he reminds the Romans, 'if we suffer with him, *in order that* we may be glorified with him' (Rom. 8:17).

Interchange of experience among Christians

It is clear that, for Paul, a present sharing in Christ's death not only means concern for others and a denial of present status, but could involve physical danger and suffering as well. The letter to the Philippians was written when Paul was in prison, facing a capital charge. He is unconcerned about the outcome – except in so far as his death would deprive his churches of his pastoral care (1:19–26). His only concern is to honour Christ, whether by his life or by his death (1:20). 2 Corinthians tells us something of the toll his missionary work was taking on him physically. He writes:

> We are in every way hard pressed, but not crushed; bewildered, but not driven to despair; hunted down, but not destroyed; we carry always in our body the death of Jesus, so that the life of Jesus may be revealed in our body; for while we live we are being handed over to death for Jesus' sake, *in order that* the life of Jesus may be revealed in our mortal flesh. So death is at work in us, but life in you. (2 Cor. 4:8–12)

Paul goes on to contrast his present, earthly, existence, with the future, heavenly one (4:16–5:10). Future death is now on the horizon – but so is a living with Christ beyond death. That future death is the logical consequence of the suffering which Paul is already enduring – suffering which is both physical and mental, for he is experiencing it in his 'mortal flesh'. 'Dying with Christ' involves real suffering. But this 'dying' leads not only to a future life with Christ, but to an experience of life in the present also – a life which, though revealed through Paul's dying, is being experienced in the lives of the Corinthians (4:10–12). Once again, we see that the pattern of 'interchange' between Christ and the believer is extended to include an interchange between the apostle and his converts.

How can this be? It is because Paul and his co-workers are conformed to the pattern of Christ, and are 'your slaves for Jesus' sake' (4:5). It is because, like Christ, they are prepared to die *in order that* others may live. Sharing daily in Christ's suffering, they bring life – *his* life – to the Corinthians.

In the opening paragraph of this letter, Paul has already spelt out how this happens:

> The God of all comfort comforts us in all our suffering, so that we are able to comfort others in all their suffering, through the comfort with which we are comforted by God. For just as the sufferings of Christ overflow in our experience, so too, through Christ, our comfort overflows also. If we are comforted, it is for your comfort – which you experience when you endure the same suffering that we experience. Our hope for you is secure, since we know that, as you share our sufferings, so you will share our comfort also. (2 Cor. 1:3–7)

Here again, we see how Paul's sufferings lead to consolation – not simply for himself, but for others, too. This is not something he himself achieves, but something that God does through him – or rather, *through Christ,* for it is because Paul is *in Christ* that this interchange of experience can take place. But just as Paul himself had to share in the sufferings of Christ and in his dying in order to experience consolation and life, so he expects the Corinthians to share in *his* sufferings (which are the sufferings of Christ).

As we shall see when we turn to 1 Corinthians, some of the Corinthians were suspicious of the role-model with which Paul had presented them. And no wonder! Putting up with suffering and hardship did not appear to be an attractive option. But Paul understood his mission to be to embody the gospel, and if his converts reject the way he lives it out, they are in effect rejecting the gospel itself.

For Paul, then, to share in the sufferings and death of Jesus is not just a question of putting up with pain and degradation and hardship, but a sharing in Christ's ministry of bringing healing and life to others. Christ himself is the source of this healing and life, but those in Christ must share in what he is, and so become those through whom this principle of 'life through death' operates. Paul, the apostle of Christ, is not unique in his calling to share

Christ's sufferings, but is the model for his converts of what 'life in Christ' means.[8]

'Interchange' means not simply that Christ suffers and dies for believers, but that they are called to suffer and perhaps die for *him*. Paul endures 'weaknesses, insults, hardships, persecutions and calamities', and because they are endured 'for Christ', he experiences the power of Christ which works through weakness (2 Cor. 12: 9–10). He sees his whole ministry as that of an ambassador, appealing on behalf of Christ that men and women will accept God's offer of reconciliation (2 Cor. 5:19–20). But he is not alone. Writing to the Philippians, he tells them that their present suffering is a 'privilege' granted to them by God: 'For the sake of Christ, you have been granted not simply to believe in Christ, but to suffer for his sake also' (Phil. 1:29). The repeated 'for the sake of Christ/for his sake' reminds us that the Philippians' suffering was a response to what he had done on their behalf. What they were experiencing was part of the same struggle that Paul himself was enduring (1:30), and like his (1:12–14) meant that the gospel was being made known to new people (1:28).

In all this, Paul is drawing out the implications of what is involved in living 'not for oneself, but for the one who died and was raised on their behalf'. If those who have died with Christ now live 'for him', then this life will bring life to others, for it is a sharing in his dying for others:

> One has died on behalf of all,
> Therefore all have died.
> And he died on behalf of all
> in order that the living might no longer live to themselves,
> but for the one who died and was raised on their behalf.
>
> (2 Cor. 5:14–15)

Life 'in Christ' is clearly not just a one-to-one relationship, but one that binds individual believers together into a single community. Christians have been made members of a single family by their baptism into Christ. Because they are *all* 'sons of God', Paul tells the Galatians, 'there is no longer Jew or Greek, no longer slave or free, no longer male and female. For you are all one in Christ Jesus' (Gal. 3:26–8). Elsewhere, he likens this community of believers to a body, whose welfare depends on the contribution made by individual members (Rom. 12:3–13; 1 Cor. 12:4–31). He also refers to the Christian community as a temple, and since the temple was regarded as God's earthly dwelling, the image is an apt one: they are God's temple because God's Spirit lives within them, and if God's Spirit lives in them, they must be holy (1 Cor. 3:16–17; 2 Cor. 6:16–18). All these images – family, body, temple – imply life, fellowship and growth, rather than an organized structure.[9]

Many of Paul's arguments begin from what he takes to be a 'given' – namely the assumption that the Holy Spirit lives within believers (Rom. 8:9; 1 Cor. 3:16; 6:19; 12:3). To live 'in Christ' means in effect that the Spirit lives in *them*. It is the Spirit who gives them life (Rom. 8:11), confirms that they are children of God (Rom. 8:14–17), and assists them in their prayers (Rom. 8:26–7). It is the Spirit who works in the lives of believers, producing the 'fruit' of holy lives, and who pours out 'spiritual gifts' on the community (1 Corinthians 12–14).

The Spirit is a 'spirit of holiness' (Rom. 1:4), and Paul regularly refers to Christians as 'saints' – literally, 'holy ones'. (2 Cor. 1:1; Phil. 1:1). This perhaps over-optimistic description reminds us that he believes Christians to be members of God's holy people, called to be holy as Israel had been. They need to live up to their calling – as Paul perhaps gently reminds them when he addresses his readers as '*called* to be saints' (Rom. 1:7; 1 Cor. 1:2).

Christian communities

He refers to the groups of Christians in various places as 'churches' or 'congregations': the Greek word *ekklēsia* means literally 'called out', and was used of an assembly of people. It was a secular term, but an obvious one for the translators of the Old Testament to adopt, and they had used it to refer to assemblies of Israel. Once again, we find Paul applying to Christians a term that has roots in the Old Testament, where God called out his people to gather to hear his commands. Hence he addresses the congregation in Corinth as 'God's *ekklēsia* in Corinth' (1 Cor. 1:2; 2 Cor. 1:1). The word refers, not to an institution, but to a community.

Paul tells us little about how the various congregations were organized. 1 Thessalonians 5:12 refers to 'those who work among you and have charge of you in the Lord and instruct you'. Among those mentioned in 1 Corinthians who contributed to the well-being of the community are prophets, teachers, and (rather low on the list!) those who helped in various ways, perhaps in administration or leadership. The terms that we associate with ministry in the church are strikingly absent. Paul never uses the term 'presbyter', and only once uses the word *episkopos,* which is usually translated as 'bishop' (Phil. 1:1). Here, the *episkopoi* and *diakonoi* (usually translated 'deacons') are linked with 'all the saints' in the letter's opening greeting. Clearly these people exercise some kind of pastoral role in the Philippian congregations, and the literal meaning of the Greek terms, 'overseers' and 'servants',[10] indicates that they had been appointed to ensure the community's integrity and spiritual and physical welfare. The more familiar translation, 'bishops and deacons', seems inappropriate when we observe that in the same sentence, Paul refers to himself and Timothy as 'slaves of Christ'. Whatever Paul is talking about, it is clearly not any kind of ecclesiastical hierarchy! It is not until we come to the Pastoral letters (1 and 2 Timothy and Titus), written in Paul's name, but almost certainly penned after his death, that we find reference to people aspiring to the office of a bishop, and instructions about how 'bishops' and 'deacons' should behave (1 Tim. 3:1–13).

The singular noun, *diakonos,* meaning literally 'servant', is used by Paul to refer to Christ – who 'became a servant of the circumcision' (Rom. 15:8) – and to himself and his co-workers, who are servants of God (1 Cor. 3:5; 2 Cor. 3:6; 6:4). Only in Philippians 1:1 and Romans 16:1 – where it is used of Phoebe – is it used of someone who may hold some kind of office in a particular Christian community.[11]

If 'structures' of ministry took time to develop, *social* structures within the Christian community were apparently slow to change. Though Paul assures the Galatians that in Christ slave and free, male and female are all equal, he did not advocate abandoning these distinctions in everyday life. Men and women must behave with due decorum (1 Cor. 11:1–16; 14:34–6), and slaves must not fret because they do not have their freedom (1 Cor. 7:21–4). In his shortest letter, written to Philemon, Paul urges him to receive Onesimus, whom he, Paul, has converted in prison, as a brother rather than a slave. Nevertheless, Onesimus is still a slave and owes a duty to his master; although Paul expresses his desire for Onesimus to return to care for him in prison, he is careful not to demand that Philemon set him free. Whether by Paul or not, the passage in Colossians 3:18–4:1 instructing wives and husbands, children and fathers, slaves and masters, how they should behave towards one another seems to accord with his views. Each group is to behave in the manner which society would have expected – but each is to do this in the way that is appropriate for those who are 'in the Lord'.[12]

If we are surprised that Paul can write a radical statement of equality such as Galatians 3:28 and then uphold the *status quo,* we have to remember, firstly, that the Christian community of Paul's day was small, insignificant and totally lacking in influence. As Paul puts it in 1 Corinthians 1:26, there were 'not many wise in human eyes, not many powerful, not many of noble birth'. The church was not yet in any position to attack social structures. Secondly, had they been able to launch an outright attack on social structures, this would have destroyed society itself and produced anarchy: the Roman world was dependent on slaves for its existence. Paul made no attempt to 'rock the boat' – perhaps realizing that the stability and ease of communications resulting from Roman rule were a positive assistance to spreading the Christian gospel. Christians should 'obey the ruling powers' and not resist them, since the authority they exercised had been given to them by God (Rom. 13:1–2). Paul's instruction to his readers in verses 6–7 that they should give to everyone what was owed to them – including taxes – is in agreement with the tradition (which may or may not have been known by Paul) that Jesus, when challenged on the question of taxes, responded by implying that Rome could legitimately demand taxes from those who used its currency (Matt. 22:15–22//Mark 12:13–17//Luke 20:20–6). Paul was clearly writing before Rome began to persecute Christians for their faith – a situation that is reflected in the book of Revelation, written somewhat later, which demonstrates a very different attitude to the Roman Empire. One wonders whether he would have written the same advice to the Roman Christians when he was in Rome itself, awaiting trial!

A third reason for Paul's 'conservative' attitude to social structures was that he wrote from the viewpoint of one who was expecting the present world order to end shortly. What that meant we must consider after we have looked more closely at how Paul believed that those who were 'in Christ' must behave.

11

'Lives worthy of the gospel'

As a Jew, Paul had been a member of a very special community. Those who belonged to it were members of a nation, but it was a nation which now had no recognized earthly leader. Although Jews in Judaea and Galilee, together with those who lived further afield – members of the Diaspora – were all ruled by Rome, nevertheless their true leader was God, and it was to him that they were answerable. Their allegiance to him was based on the belief that God had brought their ancestors out of Egypt, into the Promised Land. On Sinai he had made a covenant with them: because he loved them and had redeemed them from slavery and had called them to be his people, they promised, in response, to worship him alone and to obey his laws. This was the foundation of the relationship between God and his people – a relationship that has been aptly termed 'covenantal nomism':[1] the covenant between God and his people meant that in response to his grace, which had been demonstrated in their salvation, they willingly agreed to obey his law.

The obedience of faith

As a Christian, Paul continued to believe himself to be a member of God's people – though now that community had expanded to include Gentiles. God had once again acted to save his people – this time from the power of sin – and had called them to *be* his people. So how, now, are they to respond to his love and his grace, seen in the life, death and resurrection of Christ? Not, clearly, by obedience to the law, which Paul now views as an interim system. But certainly there must be *some* sort of response. God's people must live, act and speak like those who belong to God. Paul, the apostle to the Gentiles, describes his mission as being 'to bring about the obedience of faith among the Gentiles' (Rom. 1:5; cf. 15:18): trust in what God has done must lead to obedience. What this obedience comprises is quite simply the love for God and love for one's neighbour that the law required but which Israel had, in Paul's view, failed to demonstrate (Rom. 13:8–10; cf. Gal. 5:13–14). If, as we have seen, Christ's death has dealt with sin in order that the requirement of the law might be fulfilled in the lives of Christians, that 'fulfilling' comes about as the result of the fact they share Christ's risen life, and live according to the Spirit (Rom. 8:3–4). God's gracious act of salvation in Christ has in effect established a 'new covenant' (1 Cor. 11:25), and those who accept the terms of this covenant and are members of this new community must live in a manner that is worthy of those who belong to the Lord (1 Cor. 11:27–34). What they are now expected to obey can be described as 'the law of Christ', and it is fulfilled by those who have received the Spirit (Gal. 6:1–2).

When Paul describes Christ as the *telos* – the 'end' or 'goal' – of the law, therefore, he means not simply that Christ, rather than the law, is the supreme revelation of what God is like and that Christ, rather than the law, is the expression of his purpose for humanity and the universe. He means also that the defining mark of those who belonged to the people of God was not their obedience to the law but their obedience to Christ. And just as the law was about a way of life, so obedience to Christ is concerned with a way of life. Just as the statement 'I am the Lord your God, who brought you out of the land of Egypt, out of the house of slavery', was followed by a 'therefore . . . ' (Exod. 20:2; Deut. 5:6), so Paul's statements about what God has done through the life, death and resurrection of Jesus are followed by a 'therefore . . .' As we saw in looking at Romans, the 'therefore . . .' there involves a total transformation of the whole person into what God intended each individual to be (Rom. 12:1–2). Those who once offered themselves to sin are now, *in Christ,* able to offer themselves to God (Rom. 6:13–19; 12:1).

For Paul, there is an inexorable logic about this 'therefore'. God's commandment to Israel had been: 'You shall be holy, for I the Lord your God am holy' (Lev. 19:2), and the requirement was still that God's people should be what God – in Christ – had revealed himself to be. But Paul's appeal goes beyond requiring what is fitting. As before, it is grounded in what God has already done, but what he has done has *already* radically changed them. In Christ, Christians have already been 'washed . . . sanctified . . . righted' (1 Cor. 6:11), because Christ is the source of their righteousness and sanctification and redemption (1 Cor. 1:30). What Paul is in effect commanding them, therefore, is to *be what they already are* – in Christ.

This appeal is sometimes described as the 'indicative-imperative': Christians are commanded to be (imperative) what they already are (indicative). It arises from the fact that Paul believes that the End has in a sense already begun. Christians are *already* living in the Age to Come, but since they continue to exist in the Present Age, they need to be continually exhorted to 'be what they are', and to live up to their calling. There is only one thing that is required of you, Paul tells the Philippians, and that is that you live in a way that is worthy of the gospel (Phil. 1:27). It is the gospel – the good news – about what God has done for them that has saved them, and that gospel must now guide their behaviour.

The appeal to love

The commands to love God and their neighbour, and to live in love and harmony with one another, may not sound so very different from what had been said centuries before, but there is one essential difference. Paul is convinced that what mortals are themselves unable to achieve can in fact be achieved by the Spirit of God at work in human hearts and lives. Because Christians have died to their old life, which was dominated by sin, and now share the risen life of Christ, it is not they who obey the commands, but the Spirit working *in* them. When men and women gratify their own desires, they do 'the works of the flesh'. When they do the will of God, what they do is 'the fruit of the Spirit', since this fruit is the work of the Spirit living in them (Gal. 5:16–26).

So what did this mean, in practical terms? 'The whole law,' Paul says, 'is summed up in a single commandment, "You shall love your neighbour as yourself"' (Gal. 5:14). Earlier in that letter, he had summed up his present manner of life by declaring 'It is no longer I who live, but Christ who lives in me.' And who was this 'Christ'? None other than 'the Son of God, who loved me and gave himself up for me' (Gal. 2:20). Clearly, then, love for others and giving oneself up for others must be the hallmark of the Christian life. Paul makes repeated appeals for love. God himself is the source of love, and it is his love that saves and sustains his people (Rom. 5:5; 8:35, 39; 2 Cor. 5:14; 13:13). It is love, above all, that should characterize his people (1 Corinthians 13). They must love one another (1 Thess. 4:9–12; Rom. 13:8–10), since love binds the members of the community together and makes them a unity (Phil. 2:1–4). Those who love share the mind of Christ himself, and so reflect his attitude (Phil. 2:5–11); they 'shine like stars in the world' (Phil. 2:15), showing outsiders what God is like.

The appeal to love is an appeal to have certain attitudes. It is, however, difficult to spell out what love means in specific commands to do this or that, though naturally it includes such commandments as 'You shall not commit adultery; you shall not murder; you shall not steal; you shall not covet' (Rom. 13:9). These things are forbidden because they harm one's neighbour. But the duties of love cannot be pinned down to specific requirements. Love means being of the same mind, sharing the same love, having the same attitude as others in the community (Phil. 2:2). It means caring for the welfare of others rather than oneself, and abandoning pride in one's own achievements (Phil. 2:3). Love arises from the life of the Spirit of God, who dwells in the community, and binds it together in compassion and sympathy (Phil. 2:1).

The famous 'hymn to love' in 1 Corinthians 13 spells out what love involves. Among its characteristics, love is said to be patient and kind; it is *not* envious or boastful or arrogant or rude. Love does not insist on its own rights and is not irritable or resentful (13:4–5). This passage does not appear in 1 Corinthians by accident. A closer examination of the letter will show just how relevant this chapter is to the letter's concerns, and will give us some insight into how Paul dealt with the day-to-day problems that arose in one of his churches.

Everyday problems in Corinth

The city of Corinth was a flourishing seaport in Achaia (the southern part of Greece). It was strategically placed on a narrow isthmus of land which joined north and south, and separated east and west. All trade had to pass through it, and as a result it was a prosperous city and a thriving cultural centre. Corinth was a key position in which to plant a Christian community, and this is what Paul had done. But such a community was clearly open to many harmful influences. Not surprisingly, various problems had arisen and Paul has heard about them, either because people travelling on business have reported them to him (1:11), or because the Corinthians themselves have asked questions in a letter (7:1).

Paul's converts, mostly Gentiles, had worshipped the local gods, and may well have been accustomed to behaving in the kind of way castigated by Paul in Romans 1. Many of them would have been slaves, but the better-off among them would have been influenced by the ethos of competition and pride in personal achievement that characterized all areas of Corinthian society, whether intellectual discussion, business or sport. Converted to Christianity, the Corinthians continued to think in traditional ways. The city's strategic position meant that they had been visited not only by Paul, but also by Apollos (Acts 18:24–19:1), and possibly by Peter as well. The Corinthian Christians began to compare the abilities of the various Christian preachers and to divide into cliques, boasting about the particular leader whom they favoured (1 Cor. 1:10–17). Some of them apparently boasted in their own wisdom and maturity (1:18–2:13). In Paul's eyes, their quarrels demonstrate their immaturity (3:1–4) and are tearing the church apart, destroying the work of God's Spirit (3:10–23). Their devotion to human leaders shows that they have misunderstood the central message of the gospel (3:5–9; 4:1–21), which is not about gaining riches and glory and status in human terms, but about Christ crucified, and the call to become like him. Christians are those who 'have the mind of Christ' (2:16): it is a bold claim, but one that will be demonstrated in love for one another, and not in boasting. No wonder, then, that in 1 Corinthians 13 Paul reminds the Corinthians that understanding mysteries and having knowledge are of no value without love, which is never envious or boastful or arrogant or rude.

The Corinthians' tendency to quarrel and to assert their own opinion is demonstrated in the fact that they are going to court, not only against outsiders, but also against one another. Paul is appalled. 'Why not rather be wronged?' he asks (6:1–8). 'Why not rather be defrauded?' Better that than oppose each other in the secular courts. The Corinthians' attitudes towards one another are anything but loving. Clearly they need reminding that 'Love does not insist on its own way . . . bears all things . . . endures all things' (13:5–7).

The Corinthians needed clear guidance on sexual matters, too. One or two of them were apparently indulging in practices that would not be tolerated among pagans (5:1). Why? It would seem that they had misunderstood Paul's message about Christians being set free from sin as meaning that in their new lives sin was not a relevant concept, and that as a result they were free to behave as they wished in relation to anything that concerned their 'fleshly' existence. They could therefore have sexual intercourse with whom they wished and eat and drink to excess (6:12–13). These people were behaving as they wished, gratifying their own desires, without thought for the well-being of others. 'Everything is lawful,' they cried. 'But not everything is beneficial,' retorted Paul – that is, of mutual benefit. 'Everything is lawful' – 'but,' said Paul, 'one must not become enslaved to anything' (6:12).

It may well be that the root of the Corinthians' misunderstanding lay in Paul's own teaching. We have noted how in Romans 8 he contrasts life lived according to the flesh with life lived according to the Spirit. His point, of course, is that though Christians are still living in the flesh – i.e. they are physically alive – their way of life should be guided by the Spirit and not by earthly passions. The fact that the life that they lived 'according to the Spirit' had to be lived 'in the flesh', however, inevitably caused tensions, since Christians sometimes forgot that they were supposed to be 'dead to sin' (Rom. 6:11). Nevertheless, the way in which they behaved in terms of their *physical* bodies must also be guided by the Spirit.

The Corinthians had apparently taken note of Paul's sharp contrast between 'flesh' and 'Spirit', but interpreted it in terms of their own culture, which assumed that the antithesis was such that what happened in one sphere had no relevance to the other. If they were now living in the Spirit, they must have reasoned, this must mean that they could do what they liked 'in the flesh' – i.e. with their physical bodies – since these belonged to what was temporary, as opposed to the eternal. In reply, Paul insists that their bodies are more than mere flesh. The Greek word *soma,* usually translated 'body', is in fact impossible to translate accurately, since Paul uses it to denote the human personality – that is, the whole human being, who is able to relate to the spiritual – to God – as well as to the physical. As long as one has a physical existence, that physical existence is relevant to who one is, and cannot be ignored. How, then, Paul protests, can the Corinthians suppose that they can use the bodies that belong to Christ (since they themselves belong to Christ) to have physical relationships with prostitutes (6:15)? 'Do you not know,' he asks them, 'that your body is a sanctuary of the Holy Spirit within you?' (6:19).

By contrast, in 1 Corinthians 7, Paul has to deal with a problem that apparently arises from precisely the opposite reaction. *Some* Corinthians supposed that the spiritual life meant the *denial* of all physical pleasures, and so adopted asceticism. Their attitude is revealed in what is apparently a quotation from their letter to Paul in 1 Corinthians 7:1: 'It is well for a man not to touch a woman.' Paul's response has often been misunderstood – partly because these words have been assumed to reflect his own attitude! In fact, he cautions against it, urging each man to have his own wife, and each woman to have her own husband. One of the interesting features of this lengthy discussion on marriage is that whatever advice is given to the husband is given also to the wife, and whatever rights the husband is said to have are ascribed to the wife also. Here is full equality between the sexes! Paul calls for mutuality and consideration: this is love for others in action. This is the more remarkable, since Paul himself has no wife (7:7). Like many others in this situation, he clearly regards this as an advantage! But we should note why: it gives him more time to devote to 'the affairs of the Lord' (7:32–5), which in his case means travelling the ancient world proclaiming the Gospel. It means, too, that he is saved from concern about wife and family during the time of distress that he expects to overtake the world before the End of all things finally arrives (7:25–31). Paul's response here is partly governed by his eschatological expectations, but the chapter gives no basis whatever for the common assumption that he was a misogynist: on the contrary, he seems to go out of his way to treat women as equals.

Another problem had divided the Corinthian community, and this concerned the question as to whether or not Christians were permitted to eat meat that had been sacrificed to idols. Animal sacrifices were offered to the gods but were not totally consumed, and the meat that remained was sold in the nearby market. Here, too, as in sexual matters, there were those who gloried in freedom and those who advocated abstinence. The former group flaunted their knowledge that the gods represented by idols had no real existence, since there was only one God (8:4). Paul has to agree with them – but warns them that 'knowledge puffs up', in contrast to love, which 'builds up' (8:1). Later, in chapter 13, Paul reminds them that love is *not* puffed up (13:4). Here he insists that those who have knowledge must be careful lest their freedom from superstition, which allows them to eat this food without thereby feeling that they are acknowledging the existence of these gods, encourage those less confident than themselves to do something that they really consider to be wrong. By their knowledge the 'strong' may destroy those with weaker consciences – fellow-Christians for whom Christ died (8:11). By insisting on their rights, they sin not only against others, but against Christ himself. The yardstick for their behaviour must be love. Do they truly love their neighbours, or do they selfishly do what will please themselves (13:5)?

This means that Christians must not insist on their rights – and Paul, the apostle, who is committed to setting an example of what Christian love means, reminds the Corinthians of what he himself has done. As an apostle, he had certain rights – rights to a 'living allowance' that would cover the cost of food and lodging (9:1–6). That was obviously his due, not simply because the same principle applied in secular life (9:7), but because scripture supported it (9:8–12) and the Lord himself had decreed it (9:13–14) – a rare appeal by Paul to words of Jesus himself. But Paul had refused to be supported by the church and had worked at a trade in order to earn his own living – not because he was not a real apostle, but because he felt that he could best win people for the gospel by abandoning all privilege and getting alongside them. Like Christ himself, he deliberately gave up what he might have claimed for himself and identified himself with others, in order to save them (9:19–23). The moral is obvious: Christians should be willing to give up their rights for the sake of others.

But having affirmed that those Corinthian Christians who insist on their liberty are right in what they claim to know but wrong in what they do, Paul issues a further warning. They may destroy not only their weaker fellow-Christians but themselves (10:1–14). The Israelites, too, were arrogant and thought themselves immune to sin – but they fell into idolatry and sexual immorality (Exod. 32:1–6; Num. 25:1–2) and were punished (Exod. 32:35; Num. 25:9; 26:62). Christians must *never* accept invitations to dine in a pagan temple (a favourite way to entertain one's friends in ancient Corinth), since that is the equivalent of eating and drinking with the gods who are worshipped there – or rather, since these 'gods' have no existence, with demons, spiritual forces opposed to God, in whom Paul most certainly *did* believe (10:15–22).

Once again, Paul modifies the claim of the 'strong' Corinthians that 'everything is lawful' (10:23; cf. 6:12). While accepting their claim, he reminds them once more that 'not everything is beneficial'; moreover, 'not everything builds up' (which is what love does, 8:1). Their primary concern must be the welfare of others, not their own (10:24). There is no reason, therefore, why they should not themselves buy the meat in the market, and there is no need to ask where it came from (i.e. was it part of a sacrifice or not?) since everything belongs to God (10:25–6). Nor is there any need to ask questions about the meat if they are invited out to a meal. But if someone else is concerned because the meat has been sacrificed, then they should *not* eat it, lest they upset that other person. If no one else is upset, however, then Christians may eat what they wish – provided they do everything to *God's* glory (v. 31). Paul's own guiding principle is that of consideration for others, seeking their good and not his own (v. 33), and the Corinthians must do the same. They must imitate him, just as he imitates Christ (11:1). The ultimate appeal, therefore, is to be like Christ.

There is no straightforward answer, therefore, to the problem that had divided the Christian community in Corinth. The strong were right in declaring that pagan gods had no existence, but wrong to think that they could ignore the scruples of their fellow-Christians. What advice should Paul give? He goes back to first principles and appeals to the gospel itself – to the fact that Christ had died for all, and therefore for the weak, as well as for the strong (8:11). That must be the guide for their behaviour. They must do nothing contrary to the gospel – nothing that might destroy their fellow-Christians. The community that belonged to Christ as a result of his death and resurrection was called to be *like* him, and that meant that they must live according to the requirements of love. The particular course of action that they should adopt would vary according to the particular circumstance, but their guiding principle must be love for their neighbour.

Worship

In 1 Corinthians 11, Paul turns to various problems concerning the community's worship. First comes the question of how men and women should dress while worshipping. Because of Paul's teaching on this matter, insisting that women must cover their heads while men must be bareheaded, Paul has been maligned as a misogynist. This is a gross injustice. We have to remember that Paul, a Jew, had been brought up in a society that expected women to dress modestly, and that included covering their heads. In Greek and Roman societies, rules were not so strict, but women who did not cover their heads might well be taken to be prostitutes. It is not surprising that Paul expects Christian women to behave modestly, and not to bring the Christian community into disrepute, even though his arguments supporting this are somewhat tortuous (1 Cor. 11:2–16). Paul's judgement on this matter is clearly conditioned by the social customs and attitudes of the first century, and it is unfair to condemn him because he did not share those of the twenty-first. He certainly did not intend to lay down rules for future generations, and there is considerable irony in the fact that Paul, who insisted that Christians were living 'in Christ' and not 'under law' should have been turned into a law-giver whose teaching on this particular matter was treated for centuries as sacrosanct!

Concentration on what Paul says about women's headgear has obscured important features of his teaching. First, we note that, as in chapter 7, Paul deals with what men should wear side by side with what is appropriate for women – though here, it is true, his argument is based on the presupposition that women are in a subordinate relationship to men, a presupposition which offends the very different assumptions of today. Secondly, we must remember that women's head covering offered them protection from unwelcome attention, and so would have been seen by Paul as contributing to mutual respect and concern for other members of the Christian community. Thirdly, and most importantly, we should note that Paul assumes that women will be taking an active part in prayer and prophecy.[2] In the Jewish synagogue, women almost certainly sat apart,[3] and worship was conducted by the male members of the congregation. Paul, however, apparently takes it for granted here that women will be joining in the leading of worship by praying and preaching.[4] To do so, however, they must be properly attired – as must the men.

A second issue concerns the community's practice of gathering together to eat 'the Lord's Supper'. Paul links this specifically with the Last Supper eaten by Jesus and his disciples, and provides us with a rare fragment of tradition about Jesus' ministry: it is in fact the earliest written tradition that we possess about the Last Supper.

Paul recounts the story because the Corinthians are behaving inappropriately, breaking up into cliques. Those who arrive first eat their fill and get drunk, while latecomers get nothing. The problem may have been caused by social differences, with the well-to-do arriving first and slaves coming last.[5] Whatever the cause, one group is humiliating the other, and showing contempt for the Church of God. Once again, the law of love is being ignored. Those who eat and drink for their own satisfaction, without being aware of the needs of the whole community, are ignoring what the celebration of the Supper proclaims – the Lord's death for their sakes. Their behaviour is thus a flagrant denial of the gospel itself. Paul urges the Corinthians to wait for one another – yet another example of his demand that they show love for others (11:17–34).

Paul turns next to the issue of 'spiritual gifts'. Even this has caused problems in Corinth! The reason is that some members of the congregation claim to have been given more significant gifts than others. In first-century Corinth, spectacular gifts – such as the ability to speak in tongues or to perform miracles – were highly rated. The result was that some members of the community were boasting about their own particular gifts and despising those who did not have them. Paul reminds them that whatever gifts they have derive from the Holy Spirit, and that there are many different kinds of gift, all of which are necessary to the well-being of the community as a whole (12:1–11). Paul here uses his famous analogy of the Church as a body in which each limb and organ has a vital part to play. A body consisting entirely of eyes would be useless (and so, he implies, would be a community where the only gift was that of speaking in tongues). Each member of a body must be concerned for the others, and all must share the suffering of one member or rejoice when one member is honoured (12:12–26). Once again we have Paul insisting on the necessity for mutual concern and esteem of others within the Christian community. His next words, however, must have startled the Corinthians: 'Now you are the body of Christ', he writes (v. 27). Their relationship with Christ is so close that, together, they constitute Christ's body – his physical presence in the world, and the embodiment of his character. It is a brilliant image, for it conveys not only the reality of the relationship between Christ and individual believers, but also that between themselves. They are intimately bound together, members of a community whether they wish to be or not. As John Wesley was to say many years later: 'Christianity is essentially a social religion . . . to turn it into a solitary religion is indeed to destroy it.'[6] One cannot love God without loving one's neighbour.

From hankering after showy gifts, Paul points the Corinthians to 'a more excellent way'. It is nothing less than the way of love. Without this, the ability to speak in tongues and the gifts of prophecy, of insight into mysteries, and of knowledge are worthless (13:1–3). Love is the one essential gift – greater even than faith and hope, linked with it here as the three qualities that endure (1 Cor. 13:13; cf. 1 Thess. 1:3; 5:8; Col. 1:4–5).

It is from the viewpoint of love, therefore, that Paul now assesses the spiritual gifts which the Corinthians prize. Prophecy helps to build and encourage others, and is therefore valuable; the gift of tongues is less valuable, since it helps only the speaker; it is useful only if what is said is interpreted (14:1–25). It is clear from the lengthy discussion that Paul gives to this question that the pride of some Corinthian Christians in their ability to speak with tongues was causing Paul considerable concern. Again and again he reminds them that the measuring-rod for assessing the value of spiritual gifts and for judging all that is done in the community is the question: 'Does this build up the church?' (14:3–5, 12, 17, 26.)

In gatherings for worship, everyone who has something to offer – a hymn, a lesson, a revelation, a tongue, or an interpretation – should be allowed to do so – provided it builds up the church (14:26). The principle on which worship was conducted seems to resemble the one followed by the Society of Friends, who have no set form of worship, but who gather together in silence in the presence of God, waiting for individual members of the congregation to be stirred to speak. There appears to have been little silence in the Corinthian gatherings however! Worship there was clearly much noisier and more disorderly, since the Corinthian Christians were apparently all speaking at once. Those speaking in tongues must do so one at a time, urges Paul; there must not be too many of them, and there must be someone who can interpret what is said. Otherwise, they must be silent; speaking in tongues was self-indulgent, and of no help to others, if what was said was not understood (vv. 27–8). Prophets, too, should speak one at a time. When one of them has had his turn and someone else is inspired, the first must be silent (vv. 29–33). Women should not be speaking in church – they, too, should be silent (vv. 34–6). Since Paul has already spoken about women praying and prophesying (11:5), this command to them to keep silent is strange: Paul perhaps has a particular kind of speaking in mind here – namely the asking of questions (v. 35). Presumably – unlike the spirit-inspired prayer and prophecy mentioned in 11:5 – he believes that this does not contribute to the building-up of the community. Whatever it is that he has in mind, his chief objection is that this particular activity is 'shameful', because it is contrary to social convention (and so will bring the church into disrepute, not build it up).[7]

It is clear from 1 Corinthians that the meaning of the command to 'love one's neighbour' needs to be thought out in each situation. Its implications are far more pervasive than a simple list of prohibitions such as 'Do not kill, do not steal, do not commit adultery'. When Jesus was asked, 'Who is my neighbour?' he did not offer a definition but told a story, spelling out what loving one's neighbour meant in a particular situation (Luke 10:25–37). For Paul, too, it is necessary to think through who one's neighbour might be and what loving him or her might involve. Love for others will be shown in different ways according to the circumstances. There are, of course, certain constants – courtesy, mutual respect and concern – but the appropriate way to love one's neighbour will be affected by social convention and pressures. Sacrificed meat may be harmless in itself – but it is harmful if it destroys another's faith. Spiritual gifts come from God – but even they can be misused and so destroy the Church's unity. Men and women must not flout social convention if that will bring shame on the Church, instead of building it up. In different situations, the decisions about how to love one's neighbour will be different, but the command to love remains as the constant rule by which those decisions must be judged. It is the measuring-rod for Christian behaviour because the gospel itself is the story of God's love for us. The Christian calling is to live lives that are worthy of that gospel.

Paul's ethical judgements about how Christians should live, and about the behaviour that was appropriate in particular situations, were shaped by various influences. Whether or not he was familiar with the teaching of Jesus is a matter of dispute, though he certainly refers to teachings of the Lord on two occasions in 1 Corinthians.[8] As a Jew, he inherited certain assumptions about what was right and what was wrong, and frequently referred to scripture for a ruling (e.g. 1 Cor. 5:13; 14:34). His Greek education would have given him a knowledge of Greek philosophers, and there are parallels between his teaching and theirs which may be more than coincidence (e.g. Gal. 5:19–23). Important as these influences may have been, it was the gospel itself that provided the motivation and pattern for Christian behaviour. The gospel story was, however, open-ended. It told of what God *had* done, in Christ, but looked also towards a future Day of restoration and judgement (Romans 8; 1 Corinthians 15; 2 Cor. 5:10; Phil. 3:12–21). The approach of that Day added urgency to Paul's appeal to live holy lives (Rom. 13:11–13), and sometimes influenced his advice (1 Cor. 7:26). It is to the theme of the coming Day of salvation and judgement that we turn next.

12

'Then comes the end'

As we have seen, Paul inherited from Judaism an expectation that there would finally be a Day of Judgement, when good was rewarded and evil punished. Thereafter, the world would be restored to what God had originally intended. Paul interprets what God has done, is doing, and will do – in Christ – against this eschatological backcloth. The Day of Judgement is now understood to be the Day when Christ himself returns to earth. When he comes, the dead in Christ will be raised, and when that happens, the death that resulted from Adam's sin will be destroyed.

With so much still lying in the future, Paul emphasizes the importance of Christian hope. Christians who have already been righted by God exult in the hope of sharing the glory of God – the glory lost by Adam (Rom. 5:2). Although what Christians hope for cannot yet be seen, their hope is shared by the whole of creation, for when glory is given to the children of God, then the whole universe will be set free from futility and decay (Rom. 8:18–25).

Resurrection

This hope concerns future life. The Thessalonians, grieving for the loss of some of their number, are assured by Paul that there is no need for them to grieve for the dead, as do others who have no hope (1 Thess. 4:13). From their reaction, it would appear that they had assumed that the gospel concerned a prolongation of this present life. They seem not to have understood Paul's teaching that those who were united with Christ would share his resurrection.

Confidence that these dead Christians will rise is based on the fact that they are with Jesus, who died and rose (4:14). When Christ returns, Paul says, 'the dead in Christ will rise first', taking priority over the living (4:16).

This vital link between Christ's resurrection and that of believers is spelt out at length in 1 Corinthians 15. In this passage, Paul is correcting those who 'say that there is no resurrection of the dead' (15:12). Are these people, too, assuming that the Christian gospel concerns this life alone? It would seem so – or, at least, that they have no hope for any other kind of life. It would seem, too, that they may have found the idea of 'resurrection' difficult (15:35). It is possible that the Corinthians were familiar with the idea of the immortality of the soul (which promised a somewhat shadowy, disembodied existence) rather than that of resurrection, which Paul understood to mean resurrection to a new kind of life. It is impossible to know exactly what they believed, but Paul's response is vigorous.

Paul protests that if there is no such thing as resurrection, then Christ himself cannot have been raised – which means that the Corinthians' faith is vain, and that Christians who have died have perished. Christian hope, based on Christ's resurrection, must include hope for a life beyond this present one (1 Cor. 15:13–19).

What exactly will happen at the resurrection? That is something that Paul does not know, and which he can only attempt to describe by using the metaphorical language of Jewish apocalyptic literature – literature which claimed to reveal the secrets of God's plans for the future, and which was extremely popular in Paul's time.[1] 'The trumpet will sound, and we will be changed', he writes (1 Cor. 15:52). 'The Lord himself will descend from heaven with a command, with the cry of an archangel, and with the trumpet of God' (1 Thess. 4:16).[2] The language is the language of metaphor, but the hope it expresses is based on what has already taken place. If God has reconciled us to himself through the death of his Son, he can be relied on to save us from wrath (Rom. 5:8–11; 8:31–4; 1

Thess. 1:10; 5:9). Paul's conviction that Christ is the 'Last Adam', who reverses what the first Adam did, means that he is confident that those who 'have been joined with the likeness of his death will be joined with his resurrection' (Rom. 6:5). Christ's resurrection is not *analogous* with that of believers, but the *source* of theirs. It is this belief that Paul spells out in 1 Corinthians 15, and this is why he first reminds the Corinthians of the evidence for Jesus' resurrection (15:1–11). The whole Christian gospel is based on Christ's resurrection, and without it, that gospel is worthless (15:12–19). His resurrection was the 'first-fruits' of the resurrection of the dead, which was expected to take place at the End; since, in Adam, all die, in Christ all will be made alive (15:20–2).

In affirming Christian hope for a resurrection, Paul appeals not only to the causal link between Christ's resurrection and ours, but to what he calls 'the word of the Lord' (1 Thess. 4:15). Unfortunately we do not know what he had in mind. It is possible that he meant a word spoken through a prophet,[3] but he could well be referring to sayings which were thought to go back to Jesus himself; although we do not have a parallel to his description of what will happen when Christ comes in any of the Gospels,[4] such sayings may nevertheless have been in circulation in Paul's day. In either case, Paul is claiming divine authority for his teaching.

In 1 Thessalonians, Paul makes no attempt to explain what 'resurrection' might mean. Writing to the Corinthians, however, he feels that more explanation is required. Someone there is sure to ask 'how are the dead raised? In what kind of body will they come?' (15:35). Paul's answer emphasizes the difference between the 'body' that belongs to the present and that which belongs to the resurrected life. We have observed already that the 'body' is more than flesh, and refers to the whole person. In this present life, we know people through their physical bodies; in the resurrection life, we have to think of them as having spiritual bodies (15:36–41). So Paul begins a series of contrasts between the present, physical body (which, like a seed, is put into the ground, apparently dead) and the future, spiritual body. What is sown is perishable, while what is raised is imperishable; dishonour is exchanged for glory, weakness for power, the physical body for the spiritual body (15:42–4). This physical body derives from Adam, 'who became a living being', but the spiritual comes from Christ, 'who became a life-giving spirit', bringing life to others (15:45). Adam was made from the earth, and we bear his image, but Christ is from heaven, and we will bear his image (15:47–9).

Some of the Corinthians had perhaps been deriding Paul's teaching on resurrection, supposing that he was talking literally about the resurrection of physical bodies. Paul dismisses this idea as absurd – of course flesh and blood cannot inherit the kingdom of God (15:50). This is just as true for those who are still alive when the End arrives as for those who have died. When 'the last trumpet' sounds, there will be an immediate transformation: when the dead are raised they will be 'imperishable', and the living must become like them. Paul describes this transformation as though it meant putting on a new set of clothes: the perishable must put on what is imperishable, and the mortal must put on immortality (15:51–3). When that happens, death will finally have been defeated (15:54–7).

Paul's teaching about the future resurrection bodies of Christians has an interesting implication for his understanding of Christ's own resurrection. Since Paul's whole argument for our resurrection is founded on *Christ's* resurrection, and his conviction that, in Christ, Christians *share* in his resurrection and will be conformed to his image – the image, that is, of the man from heaven – we see that Christ's own resurrection body must have been spiritual, not physical. Everything that he says in 1 Corinthians 15:35–55 about the contrast between the 'mortal, perishable' body and the 'immortal, imperishable' body derives from the contrast between the first Adam, who was created from earth, and the last Adam, who is 'from heaven'. If 'flesh and blood cannot inherit the kingdom of God, nor what is perishable inherit the imperishable' (15:50), then Christ himself, at *his* resurrection, must have put on what is imperishable instead of flesh and blood. Paul could not have stressed more firmly than he does the importance of belief in Christ's resurrection, and this resurrection can certainly be described as a *bodily* resurrection; but it is a spiritual body, not a physical one, that Paul has in mind.

A change of perspective

Paul returns to the topic of Christian hope for the future once again in 2 Corinthians 5. This time, his discussion arises out of the situation he himself is facing, rather than out of difficulties raised by the Corinthians. In chapter 4, he has explained how his call to 'proclaim Jesus Christ as Lord' and to be a 'slave' of the Corinthians for the sake of Jesus has resulted in hardship and suffering (vv. 5, 7–12). He has described himself as 'carrying in the body the death of Jesus', and as 'always being given up to death for the sake of Jesus' (vv. 10–11). His missionary work has taken a considerable physical toll on him, so that he speaks of his 'outer man' decaying; yet the inner (man) is being renewed day by day (v. 16). Paul's use of the word 'man' gives us the key to his thought. The 'outer man' is his physical existence, inherited from Adam, the inner the new, spiritual existence he has from being in Christ. We have here once again the contrast between life in this age and in the age to come, between the physical and spiritual bodies of 1 Corinthians 15:42–9, between what is mortal and perishable and what is immortal and imperishable.

In 2 Corinthians 5, Paul speaks of exchanging his earthly house – a tent – for a heavenly one (v. 1). The reference to a tent points to the impermanence of earthly existence; the heavenly dwelling, in contrast, is eternal. Paul now changes the metaphor, and speaks again of 'putting on' and 'taking off', as though he were talking about changing clothes (vv. 2–4). Since he knows that God has prepared this new 'house' for him, he is sure that he will not be left 'naked' – i.e. without a body of any kind. How can he be so confident? God has given him the Spirit, he says, as a guarantee that this will happen (v. 5). The word he uses for 'guarantee' is one used in everyday Greek of a 'down-payment' or first instalment. The presence of the Spirit in his life is the sign that he has already begun to experience this new kind of existence.

Paul makes no reference here to the return of Christ or to a future resurrection. He speaks, instead, as though exchanging the temporary, earthly 'tent' for the eternal, heavenly dwelling will happen at his death, the completion of a process of decay and renewal that has already begun (4:16). Some scholars suggest that Paul has changed his understanding of what will happen since writing 1 Corinthians 15, and now expects to receive a 'resurrection body' as soon as he dies, rather than having to wait for Christ's return, as 1 Corinthians 15:23 might suggest. In 2 Corinthians 5, he contrasts being 'at home in the body' – i.e. in the physical body – with being 'away from the body and at home with the Lord' (v. 8). Has Paul abandoned the belief in a future resurrection that he affirmed so vigorously in 1 Corinthians? That could hardly be the case!

It would perhaps be fairer to speak of Paul's views *developing* rather than *changing*. Certainly his perspective has changed, for he now sees a real possibility that he may die very soon – i.e. *before* Christ's return – whereas earlier, he had assumed that he would still be alive when this took place (1 Cor. 15:51–2). He is very conscious of something about which he reminds his readers in Rome – that salvation is nearer than when they first believed (Rom. 13:11). This leads him to think through, in 2 Corinthians 4 and 5, his understanding of what being overtaken by death will involve: it will involve change, as in 1 Corinthians, but the change seems to take place at death, rather than at the Lord's return. Even though Paul's perspective may have shifted, however, the idea that the dead are 'at home with Christ' seems to have been part of his hope from the beginning, since when he wrote 1 Thessalonians (possibly his earliest letter), he assured the Thessalonians that God would 'bring with him those who had died', and then immediately went on to explain that when Christ arrived, 'the dead in Christ' would rise first. This conviction that the dead are 'with Christ' remained with Paul throughout his life, for in Philippians, facing the possibility of death, he wonders whether a death-sentence might not be preferable to release. Although his experience of Christ in this life is so close that he declares that for him 'to live is Christ', he nevertheless believes that 'to die is gain'. And so he tells the Philippians that he longs 'to depart and be with Christ', even though he knows that 'to remain in the flesh is more necessary' for them (Phil. 1:21–4). Here too, however, we find Paul affirming, a little later, that his aim was 'to attain the resurrection of the dead' (Phil. 3:11). Clearly Paul does not consider his expectation of future resurrection and his conviction that death means being 'with Christ' to be incompatible.

It is clear that Paul's hope for the future rested on his conviction that the bond between Christ and believers could not be broken by death. Those who were 'in Christ' would not be separated from him by death, and since they no longer have fleshly bodies, they must be 'with him'. But Paul was also convinced that Christ would one day exercise the authority that had been given him by God (Phil. 2:9–11), and that he would return to reign (Phil. 3:20–1; 1 Cor. 15:23–8). When that happened, then what was already a reality in heaven would become a reality on earth.

Paul attempts to describe this event in different ways. In Romans 8, he speaks of 'the revelation of the sons of God', which means our 'adoption, the redemption of our bodies' (vv. 19–23). It is a different way of speaking about the transformation that he describes in 1 Corinthians 15. When men and women become what God intended, then creation itself will be set free and restored (Rom. 8:20–2). Both Romans 8 and 1 Corinthians 15, then, speak of the ultimate triumph, while 2 Corinthians 4 and 5 express Paul's confidence that in the meantime, the Christian dead are 'with

Christ'. The idea that eschatology is not entirely future, but can in a sense be realized, applies to the life beyond this one, as well as to the present.

Judgement

There is one final aspect of the End that we must consider. The expected Day was, we have said, understood in Judaism to be the Day of Judgement. Paul shared that expectation, and so in Romans 2:16 he speaks of 'the day when God, through Christ Jesus, will judge the secret thoughts of all'. For those who have been righted by God, and who live in Christ, sharing his righteousness, such a day should hold no terrors. 'If we have been righted by Christ's death,' Paul assured the Romans, 'we shall certainly be saved through him from wrath. If we have been reconciled to God through the death of his Son, we shall certainly be saved by his life' (Rom. 5:9–10). Yet for those who are continually summoned to 'be what they are' and whose faith is expected to be demonstrated in obedience, there is always the possibility of failure. If this had not been so, Paul would not have been quite so agitated when writing to some of his churches!

References to future judgement occur from time to time in Paul's letters. He prays that the Philippians may be 'pure and blameless' on the day of Christ (Phil. 1:10). Writing to the Corinthians, he seems less confident about their fate: those who enter a race do not all win the prize, and the Corinthians need to put all their endeavours into running this particular race (1 Cor. 9:24). Paul recognizes that there is even a possibility that, after proclaiming the gospel to others, he himself may be disqualified (v. 27). It is an image he uses again, in Philippians 3:12–14, pointing out that he has not yet reached his goal. The Corinthians' arrogance may well lead them into disaster (1 Cor. 10:1–13). Paul has already exercised discipline on one member of the Corinthian community, in hope that he will be saved on the day of the Lord (1 Cor. 5:1–5). Others are eating and drinking judgement on themselves because of their selfish behaviour at the Lord's Supper, and will be judged by the Lord (1 Cor. 11:29–32). Paul himself, as a 'servant' of Christ, was answerable to him, and expected to be judged by the Lord when he came (1 Cor. 4:1–5).

God's righteous people must be righteous, urged Paul, and that meant that they were required to live out the gospel. They had indeed been righted by God, but might still fall away. The Christian's aim must always be to please the Lord. 'For we must all appear before the judgement seat of Christ,' writes Paul, 'in order that each may receive recompense for what has been done by means of the body, whether good or evil' (2 Cor. 5:9–10).

Yet Paul is confident that on that final Day, all will be well, since God will not permit his work to be in vain. Those whom he has reconciled to himself through the death of his Son can be confident that he will save them on the day of wrath (Rom. 5:9–10). In the triumphant conclusion to his vision of a restored universe, in which the children of God will once again reflect his glory, he writes:

> Who will bring a charge against God's elect?
> It is God who acquits[5] us!
> Who will condemn us?
> It is Christ who died – and more, who was raised,
> who is at God's right hand
> who intercedes for us!. . .
> I am convinced that neither death nor life,
> neither angels nor rulers,
> neither powers, nor height nor depth
> nor any other creature
> shall be able to separate us from the love of God which is in Christ
> Jesus our Lord.
>
> (Rom. 8:33–4, 38–9)

Epilogue: interpretation and misinterpretation

Any great teacher will find that his or her sayings are studied, treated with reverence, explained, interpreted, developed – and misunderstood. Not surprisingly, this is what happened to Paul.

The process began almost immediately. Within the New Testament itself, we already have 'disciples' of Paul, writing in his name after his death, endeavouring to interpret his teaching for their own time. Some scholars suggest that Colossians is an example of this process, but it reads more like a development of his thinking by Paul himself, as he attempted to work out the implications of the idea that Christ was the 'end' – i.e. the 'goal' – of the law and the true expression of God's wisdom. The letter to the Ephesians, however, is probably *not* Pauline, though it seems to have been written by someone who knew all Paul's writings well, and who used Colossians as a model. It was certainly written later than the other epistles, for Jews and Gentiles are now said to be one community, and 'the dividing wall' of hostility between the two groups has been broken down (2:14). The law has been abolished (2:15) – something Paul himself had refused to say of it (Rom. 3:31). The letter stresses the unity of the church, and elaborates some of Paul's imagery.

2 Thessalonians may well have been written by Paul himself, for it is similar in language and format to 1 Thessalonians, but it is thought by many to have been composed by someone writing in

his name; if so, then it is another attempt to adapt his teaching to a changed situation. The Pastoral letters, on the other hand, were clearly written by someone other than Paul, for their language, style and approach are very different from his. Nevertheless, they may contain genuine fragments of Pauline letters. Addressed to individuals, these letters demonstrate an interesting shift, for the author is now concerned to defend 'the faith' (1 Tim. 4:1,6) and to protect it from false teaching; he obviously believed that he was interpreting Paul's teaching for the changed situation in which he found himself. The church is now structured, and instructions are given about 'bishops and deacons' (1 Tim. 3:1–13), about the behaviour expected from women, who are to learn in silence and not teach a man! (1 Tim. 2:9–15), and about the care of widows (5:3–16). Though the letters urge their recipients to keep 'the faith', and to teach 'sound doctrine' (2 Tim. 4:3), the content of the faith is conveyed in short summaries only (1 Tim. 2:5–6; 3:16; 2 Tim. 2:11–13), and the bulk of the letters concerns discipline and order within the community. The author is concerned to advocate right belief and right action, and though these can be seen as legitimate concerns, one misses the emphasis on personal trust and response to God's grace that was so important for Paul.

Authoritative writings

Paul's letters were certainly valued by some, at least, of those who received them, or they would not have been preserved. But we have evidence that they were found puzzling by some of their readers, and misunderstood by others. The author of 2 Peter supports his own teaching by a reference to Paul:

> So, too, our beloved brother Paul wrote to you, according to the wisdom given to him, speaking about these things in all his letters. In them there are some things that are hard to understand,

> which the ignorant and unstable twist to their own destruction – as they do the other scriptures. (2 Pet. 3:15–16)

Paul's letters are here being treated as 'scripture', and so as authoritative for the Christian community.[1] Once they were recognized as part of the 'canon' of Christian scripture, and were therefore treated as authoritative, the danger that they would be treated as 'law' increased. The instructions that Paul had given in dealing with a particular problem in a particular situation were seen as having validity for all time. This danger has continued down to the present, for some Christians ignore the fact that he was writing in the first century AD and was addressing particular situations, and assume that what Paul said then still has validity today. A ludicrous example of this misuse of Paul was the obligation felt by women for centuries to cover their heads in worship because first-century custom led Paul to decree it; a more significant one was the refusal to allow women to teach or exercise authority in the Church because someone writing in Paul's name had once forbidden them to do so. Seizing on what was forbidden in 1 Timothy, people ignored Paul's radical teaching about the equal status of women in God's sight, and as a result he was unfairly labelled a misogynist.

An even more tragic example of the unfortunate consequences of assuming that the teaching Paul gave in one context must be followed slavishly by future generations living in very different situations was seen in the way that many German Christians failed to resist the Nazis in the 1930s because Paul had instructed the Romans to be subject to the ruling authorities (Rom. 13:1–7). Paul would certainly have been horrified at his teaching being treated in this legalistic way.

It is arguable, too, that Christians failed for centuries to do anything about the slave trade because Paul accepted the *status quo* existing in his day. It was surely a gross *mis*interpretation of

Paul's teaching to suppose that what he said about how one should behave *within* a particular social system gave approval *to* that social system for all time.[2] It was surely a gross misinterpretation also, at the same time to *ignore* his teaching about the need for love and concern for others. As we saw in looking at his teaching on ethics (above, chapter 11), Paul appealed to basic principles – love, concern for others – and tried to apply them in particular circumstances. Those circumstances inevitably shaped the advice he gave. Had the Christian world taken his basic teaching about love seriously, social legislation to deal with exploitation would have been introduced centuries before reformers first succeeded in doing so, slavery would have been abolished, and women would have been accorded their rightful place in the Christian community.[3]

The break with Judaism

Another change that took place after Paul's death had a great effect on the way that Paul was read. In the early days of the Church, as we have seen, 'Christianity' was a sect *within* Judaism, which meant that Christians had to explain themselves and their beliefs to their fellow-Jews. It was Christians who were regarded as the unorthodox, the schismatics, the 'heretics'. But Paul's own work had pushed the gospel out into the gentile world, and soon there were more Gentiles than Jews who had responded to the gospel. Although Paul insisted that gentile Christians had been 'grafted' into the parent tree – i.e. Israel – it was inevitable that Christians would in time break away from Judaism. As Jewish Christians were forcibly evicted from synagogues, and gentile Christians were shunned by Jews, the communities grew apart. Christians met separately to worship God, and moved away from their Jewish roots. After Paul's death, opposition between Jews and Christians intensified, until eventually the break between them was finalized.

When Paul's letters were re-read in this bitter atmosphere, what had been part of a 'family feud', where common assumptions were taken as read, now seemed to have a more sinister tone. Paul's arguments about the inability of the law to fulfil its promises were understood to be a condemnation of the law itself. Paul, Jewish to his fingertips, who had agonized about the failure of his people to accept the gospel (Rom. 9:1–5) and who had insisted that God would save them (Romans 9–11), was now seen as opposed to all things Jewish. One second-century teacher, Marcion, totally ignoring Paul's Jewish roots, interpreted his teaching as an attack on Judaism. Paul's teachings were distorted to provide authorization for anti-Semitism and persecution of the Jews. This was the worst and most tragic misinterpretation of all.

With this shift from Christians-within-Judaism to 'Christianity' came, too, a shift from the emphasis on the communal to the personal. While Paul agonized about whether Israel would be saved, later generations were far more concerned about the salvation of individuals. By the time of the Reformation, we find Luther laying great emphasis on 'justification by faith', but ignoring what Paul said about the salvation of Israel. As a result, Luther's emphasis on faith over against 'works' – now reinterpreted to mean acts that were believed to give an individual 'merit', rather than 'the works set out in the law' – became not just the rallying-cry of Protestants against Catholics, but a defence of 'Gospel' against 'Law', and so of 'Christian' against 'Jew'. Judaism was now seen as a legalistic religion, and was understood to be based on the assumption that one could earn salvation by obedience to the law, in contrast to Christianity, which was seen as a religion of grace.[4]

Paul has sometimes been accused of misunderstanding and misinterpreting Judaism. It is perhaps fairer to say that he himself has been misunderstood because he has not been seen in the context of his time, and in terms of what he was endeavouring to do.

But can we be confident that we have truly understood him? It would be a foolish exegete who made such a claim! It is impossible for anyone to enter fully into the mind of another person, and in the case of Paul we are dealing with a remarkable man, who lived in a very different culture from our own, and who was attempting to bring together his long-held beliefs about the nature and purposes of God with his new conviction that this God had revealed himself in the life, death and resurrection of Christ. The vast number of books that pour from the printing presses is some indication of the very different interpretations given to his thinking. In the past hundred years, for example, he has been explained as someone who belonged to the Hellenistic world, and who interpreted the gospel in the language and thought-forms of the Greeks,[5] and as someone who was thoroughly Jewish in his thinking and his approach[6] – the view advocated in this book.[7]

In the course of this book, we have noted disagreements among scholars about matters such as Paul's Christology, his attitude to the law, and his understanding of the death of Christ. There have been disagreements, too, about what is the central 'core' of Paul's theology: was it 'justification by faith' – the view that dominated Protestant exegesis in the centuries following Luther[8] – or was it the idea of 'being-in-Christ' – an idea explored in a famous book by Albert Schweitzer.[9] The former idea is prominent in Romans and Galatians, but not elsewhere: is the debate about 'justification by faith' perhaps more to do with the question of the relation between Jews and Gentiles than with the question of *how* one is saved?[10] Or should we perhaps say that 'justification' – or 'righteousness' – 'faith' and 'being-in-Christ' are perhaps *all* different aspects of Paul's understanding of a gospel that was fundamentally about what God had done, in Christ, to reconcile the world to himself (2 Cor. 5:19)?

New methods of biblical interpretation bring new insights into Paul's thought. There have been important developments in the attempt to understand Paul in his own social context and culture, rather than view him in terms of our own cultural presuppositions.[11] Social-scientific approaches,[12] rhetorical criticism,[13] and narrative criticism[14] have all made a contribution to the attempt to see Paul within his own thought-world. Feminist criticism,[15] too, has shed new light on the Pauline letters, reminding those accustomed to reading Paul through the eyes of male commentators of the important role played by women in the Pauline communities.

Paul's 'arrogance'

One accusation often brought against Paul is that he taught a totally different gospel from that proclaimed by Jesus himself. He has been described, for example, as the *real* founder of Christianity. At first sight it does indeed seem that the message of Jesus was very different from Paul's. But we have to remember that while Jesus taught about God, not about himself,[16] Paul, too, who is apparently so Christocentric in his teaching, is concerned primarily with what *God* did *through* Christ. Jesus did not come to 'found' a new religion, but to call his people back to God. But Paul, also, was not founding a 'new religion', for he saw his gospel as the fulfilment of God's promises, and his mission was to call Gentiles to *join* God's people. If Paul's gospel centres on the death and resurrection of Jesus, that was an inevitable shift for any Christian after Easter: neither of these events could be ignored! Christ's death demanded explanation, while his resurrection proved to be the mind-shattering event that created faith. 'The proclaimer became the proclaimed', not because his gospel was being put aside, but because what Jesus had done and said were being affirmed. What Jesus had announced in terms of the Kingdom of God (already present, in him, and yet still to come), Paul now proclaimed as the righteousness of God (already present in Christ, yet still to be established). Although Paul's contribution to Christianity was enormous, his understanding of the gospel was not a distortion of Jesus' own message and mission.

Hand in hand with the idea that Paul saw himself as founding a new religion goes the accusation that he was arrogant and authoritarian. It is his letters to the Corinthians in particular that are used in evidence against him, but already in Galatians we see Paul arguing with Peter and setting him straight (Gal. 2:11–21)! His reason, of course, is that he considers Peter's action to be a denial of the gospel they both believe in, and he is not afraid to say so. When we turn to 1 and 2 Corinthians we see that here, too, what seems like a defence of himself is always a defence of the gospel. He defends attacks on his lifestyle by showing how it conforms to the gospel itself (1 Cor. 4:1–16; 2 Cor. 4:7–15); to behave differently, he implies, would be to deny the gospel. He denies that he has been fickle in his dealings with the Corinthians: on the contrary, he has been trustworthy, as God himself is trustworthy (2 Cor. 1:17–24). He compares his own ministry with that of Moses – a bold claim indeed for a Jew! – but only because Moses reflects the glory of Sinai, while his own task is to reflect the even greater glory of Christ (2 Cor. 3:1–4:6). He defends himself, but only in order to defend the gospel, for if he is not an apostle, then his message is invalid (1 Cor. 9:1–2; 2 Cor. 3:1–3).

It is in 2 Corinthians 10–13 that Paul appears to be most argumentative and arrogant. These chapters are so different in tone from the preceding ones that they are thought by many to be part of another letter – possibly the letter written in anguish and with tears referred to in 2 Corinthians 2:4. Whatever their origin, they were clearly intended to deal with a crisis in the Corinthian church – a crisis brought about because Paul's authority was being denied. Paul was certainly in a difficult situation: he needed to defend himself, but was well aware that he would inevitably sound arrogant. 'It is necessary to boast,' he says (2 Cor. 12:1) – though he knows that to do so is foolish. But how else is he to persuade the Corinthians that he is indeed an apostle, in spite of what his detractors say? Paul is embarrassed by the whole affair. 'Do you think we have been defending ourselves?' he asks (2 Cor. 12:19).

He has, of course, been doing precisely that, but 'everything is for the sake of building you up'. How can what he says do that if they do not accept his authority?

It is easy to distort Paul's teaching by reading him out of context, and to picture him as a disagreeable, arrogant man, for ever arguing with others, and defending his own rights and privileges. He does, indeed, do that – in 1 Corinthians 9 – but only to explain that he has renounced these privileges! How typically awkward, we think, until we realize that it is only by appealing to the Corinthians to imitate his example (11:1) that he can get them to understand what living out the gospel means. His problem is precisely that he does not see his call to be Christ's apostle as a call to enjoy status and honour, but as a call to be the means of revealing God's Son to the Gentiles. In the Corinthian world, the apostle who accepted honour and privilege did not need to defend himself, because his position and authority were obvious to others. It is the apostle who willingly accepted suffering and dishonour who was forced to defend himself by reminding his readers that this was what the gospel of Christ crucified was about. The irony is that as a result, he has continued to be the recipient of calumny and to be slandered as arrogant.

To understand Paul, we need to endeavour to see him, as far as is possible, in terms of his own time and situation, and to ask why he felt so passionately about his calling and why he reacted as he did. The man whose thinking we have been exploring in these pages was undoubtedly a profound thinker, whose understanding of the Christian gospel – though often, sadly, misunderstood – was of tremendous importance for later theology and spirituality. Paul wrestled with the intricacies of God's purpose in history, his self-revelation in his Son, and above all the implications of Christ's death and resurrection for the everyday life of the believer. If he is ignored and abused today, he would not be surprised! He suffered far worse in his own day. But he surely deserves to be accorded the status that he would never have claimed, and recognized as the greatest and the most influential of all Christian theologians.

Endnotes

Chapter 1

1. Acts is traditionally attributed, together with the Gospel clearly written by the same author, to Luke, who is mentioned several times in Paul's letters. There is no way of establishing whether or not the tradition is true, but there is no particular reason to dispute it. It is convenient – and possibly accurate! – to refer to the author as 'Luke'.
2. 2 Cor. 12:7.
3. Deut. 23:1. Contrast the promise of future inclusion in Isa. 56:3–5.
4. The contrast between 'Jews' and 'Hellenists' in this passage indicates that the latter term must refer here to Greek-speaking Gentiles.
5. Traditions about what was said are likely to be less reliable than traditions about what was done.
6. The words in square brackets are generally assumed to be Paul's own.
7. For a discussion of its meaning, see pp. 77–9.
8. A similar example of language which, though unusual, turns out to be highly appropriate, is found in 1 Thessalonians 1:10. Although this is understood by many to be a summary of the gospel, it is a somewhat inadequate one! It is better understood as a summary of the themes that Paul intends to discuss later in the letter. See M. D. Hooker, '1 Thessalonians 1.9–10: a Nutshell – but What Kind of Nut?' in *Geschichte – Tradition – Reflexion,* Festschrift für Martin Hengel zum 70. Geburtstag, Volume III Frühes Christentum, ed. H. Lichtenberger (Tübingen: J.C.B. Mohr (Paul Siebeck), 1996), pp. 435–48.
9. Col. 3:16.
10. See pp. 113, 119, 121–2, 128–9.
11. Rom. 1:4; 10:9; 1 Cor. 12:3; Phil. 2:11.
12. 1 Cor. 7:10–11. Cf. Matt. 5:31–2; 19:3–9; Mark 10:2–12; Luke 16:18.
13. 1 Cor. 9:14. Cf. Matt. 10:1–15; Mark 6:7–11; Luke 9:1–5; 10:1–12. Interestingly, however, Paul clearly does not consider himself bound by this instruction!

14. Rom. 14:14. Cf. Mark 7:18.
15. 1 Thess. 4:15–17. Cf. Matt. 24:30–31.

Chapter 2

1. The term 'apostle' is derived from a Greek verb meaning 'to send', and refers to someone who has been entrusted with a particular commission.
2. See, for example, C. K. Barrett, *The Acts of the Apostles,* Vol. 1, ICC (Edinburgh: T. & T. Clark, 1994), pp. 671f.
3. 1 Cor. 9:1; cf. Rom.1:1; 1 Cor. 1:1; 2 Cor. 1:1; Gal. 1:1. For Luke, the eleven + one apostles were witnesses to Jesus' resurrection (Acts 1:22), while Paul's experience on the Damascus road took place *after* the ascension, which marked the departure of the risen Lord into heaven. It is perhaps significant that, in all three accounts of this experience, Luke describes Paul as having seen a light, rather than the Lord (Acts 9:3–4; 22:6–7; 26:13–14). Nevertheless, Luke understands Paul to be, in his own way, a 'witness' to the resurrection: see 17:22–32; 23:6; 26:8.
4. Having made the point in Acts chapter 14, however, he never uses the term for Paul and Barnabas again. In spite of his admiration for Paul, it would seem that he thought of the original group of twelve as 'the apostles'.
5. Cf. the references to 'signs and wonders' in Acts 2:22 and 43. Luke includes accounts of healings by the apostles which mirror some of the miracles of Jesus; see Acts 3:1–10; 9:36–43.
6. They perform 'signs and wonders' in Acts 14:3 and 15:12. A similar point is also made about Stephen, 6:8. Cf. 14:8–10; 16:16–18; 20:7–12. For Paul himself, such signs and wonders were the mark of being a true apostle, 2 Cor. 12:12; cf. Rom. 15:18–19.
7. Acts 9:1–19; 22:3–21; 26:4–18.
8. Luke 9:51–3; 13:31–3; 18:31–4.
9. It is noticeable that Luke's Gospel begins (Luke 1:5–23) and ends (Luke 24:52–3) in Jerusalem. Jesus pays two visits there as a child (2:22–51), and his resurrection appearances take place in or near Jerusalem (Luke 24: contrast Luke 24:6 with Mark 16:7. Matt. 28:10–20 and John 21:1–24, like Mark, associate resurrection appearances with Galilee).

10. Rom. 15:25–8; 1 Cor. 16:1–4; 2 Cor. 8–9.
11. Rom. 1:1; 1 Cor. 1:1; 2 Cor. 1:1; Gal. 1:15–16.
12. Rom. 1:5; 15:15–16; Gal. 1:16; 2:7.
13. Most scholars believe that Mark was the first Gospel to have been written, and that it was used by Matthew and Luke; some think that Luke drew on Matthew as well, but it is more generally supposed that Matthew and Luke both drew on a common source or sources (known as 'Q'). Such similarities as exist between Luke and John are variously explained as the result of John drawing on Luke, Luke drawing on John, or independent use by the two authors of parallel traditions.
14. 'We' occurs at various points in the following passages: Acts 16:10–17; 20:5–8, 13–15; 21:1–18; 27:1–8, 15–20, 27–9, 37; 28:1–16.
15. God-fearers were Gentiles who attended the local synagogue, but who had not formally converted to Judaism.
16. The phrase 'after three years' could mean a full three years, but might also mean a period *between* two and three years, so the total time-span (3 + 14) may have been less than it appears to us. It is sometimes argued that Paul is dating *both* intervals from his conversion, which would make the period even shorter.
17. It is sometimes argued that Paul could not have been trained by Gamaliel because in Galatians 1:22 he denies that he was known to the Christians in Jerusalem. In Galatians 1:17–24, however, Paul's purpose is to insist that he did not visit Jerusalem in the early years *after* his conversion; he is not concerned there with the period *before* that event.
18. Acts 18:3. Tents would probably have been made of leather, but tent-makers also made awnings to keep off the glare of the summer sun, and these would have been made of linen. See Jerome Murphy O'Connor, *Paul: A Critical Life* (Oxford and New York: OUP, 1997), pp. 85–9.
19. 1 Cor. 4:12; 9:4–18; 1 Thess. 2:9; cf. Acts 20:34.
20. Acts 7:58; 8:1,3; 9:1–30; 22:4–5; 26:9–12.
21. 1 Cor. 15:9; Gal. 1:13, 23; Phil. 3:6.
22. It is often suggested that Luke presents Paul here as a member of the Jerusalem Sanhedrin. This may have been Luke's understanding, but the word 'sanhedrin' refers to a court or council, and did not necessarily denote a fixed or permanent body. It has been strongly argued that

there was no such permanent body or Sanhedrin in the first century AD. See Martin Goodman, *The Ruling Class of Judaea* (Cambridge: CUP, 1987), pp. 112–6; E.P. Sanders, *Judaism: Practice and Belief 63 BCE*–66 CE (London: SCM/Philadelphia: TPI, 1992), pp. 472–88.

23. John 18:31 states that the Jewish authorities were not permitted to put anyone to death, but the accuracy of this statement is much debated by historians. Acts records not only the death of Stephen (7:54–60), but that of James also (at the hands of Herod (12:2–3)).
24. The punishment decreed in Deuteronomy 25:2–3 was forty lashes; in practice this became 39, in case a mistake was made and the number was exceeded.
25. Rom. 1:1; 1 Cor. 1:1; 2 Cor. 1:1; Gal. 1:1.
26. It is Luke, once again, who gives us this location.
27. Most English versions translate this phrase 'to me', but the Greek preposition *en* used here means primarily 'in', not 'to'.
28. 2 Cor. 1:19–20.
29. The case for beginning with Paul's letters was famously made by John Knox, *Chapters in a Life of Paul* (New York: Abingdon-Cokesbury, 1950).
30. Similar points are made in Romans 1:5–6 and 15:15–20, where Paul is setting out his credentials to a Christian community that he has not founded. In the latter passage, he also explains his mission strategy.
31. This belief is based on 1 Corinthians 15:32 and 2 Corinthians 1:8. In the former passage, Paul speaks of having 'fought with wild beasts at Ephesus', but these are surely metaphorical. In the latter, he refers to a serious affliction that overtook him in Asia: 'We were so utterly burdened – far beyond our strength – that we despaired of life itself. But we received in ourselves the sentence of death, so that we should no longer trust in ourselves, but in God who raises the dead.' The danger is unspecified: it may well have been serious illness or mob violence.

Chapter 3

1 A fourteenth, Hebrews – which is not, in fact, a letter (see note 10) – was also traditionally attributed to Paul, but makes no claim to have been written by him. Like the Gospels, it is anonymous. It was probably because it was thought to be by Paul, however, that it was

included in the New Testament canon, since apostolic authorship was considered to be a guarantee of a book's reliability.

2. The same list (in a different order) was given earlier by Marcion, an influential second-century Gnostic, whose writings are often thought to have given the impetus to creating the New Testament canon. Church Fathers such as Irenaeus, Clement of Alexandria and Origen, on the other hand, seem to have known and used *all* the Pauline epistles.
3. Collections were probably made much earlier. The reference in 2 Pet. 3:15–16 to what Paul had said 'in all his letters', describing them as 'scripture', suggests that collections had been made much earlier than AD 200.
4. 2 Thessalonians is also missing. The manuscript is, however, incomplete, lacking the first seven and the last seven sheets. It begins at Rom. 5:17 and ends with 1 Thessalonians. There would have been room to include 2 Thessalonians, but not the Pastorals.
5. See Galatians 6:11; 2 Thess. 3:17. Cf. also Rom. 16:22, where Tertius identifies himself as the scribe who wrote the letters.
6. 1 Tim. 4:6; 6:1, 3; 2 Tim. 1:13–14; Tit. 1:9; 2:1.
7. 1 Tim. 1:15; 2:5; 3:16; 2 Tim. 2:11–13; Tit. 3:4–8a.
8. A. Q. Morton and James McLeman, *Paul, the Man and the Myth* (London: Hodder & Stoughton, 1966).
9. E.g. many of the letters are too short to provide sufficient information; Paul's extensive use of Old Testament quotations could easily upset their statistics; the authors' own statistics contained many anomalies, which they sometimes chose to ignore.
10. The so-called 'Letter to the Hebrews', which *is* a theological treatise, is *not,* in fact, a letter. It does, however, *end* like a letter, and may be an exposition which was sent by its author to a community in his pastoral care.
11. The opening words of his novel *The Go-Between.*

Chapter 4

1. See Rom. 16:20; 1 Cor. 5:5; 7:5; 2 Cor. 2:11; 11:14; 12:7; 1 Thess. 2:18. He uses an alternative name, Beliar, in 2 Cor. 6:15.
2. A clear example of this is Paul's condemnation of homosexual practice (see Rom. 1:26–7), which was regarded as abhorrent by Jews

(Lev. 18:22; 20:13), but was tolerated, even admired, in the Greek world.

3. The term 'torah', meaning 'teaching' or 'instruction', was translated in the Septuagint by the Greek word *nomos,* meaning 'law', and this is the term commonly used by Paul. This illustrates one of the problems of translation: a word in one language rarely corresponds exactly with a single word in another. In this case, 'law' is the nearest English equivalent to the Greek *nomos,* and since Paul himself employs the word *nomos,* and 'law' often seems to be a better translation than 'teaching', the word 'law' has generally been used in what follows. Torah is more than 'law', however – though the covenant-law lies at its core. In using the term *nomos* Paul appears sometimes to be thinking of the laws on Sinai, and sometimes to be using it as the equivalent of 'scripture'. On occasion I have used the word 'Torah' rather than 'law', in order to underline the fact that the Hebrew scriptures are more than what would normally be described as 'law'.
4. These five books, known also as the Pentateuch, and sometimes referred to as the five books of Moses, contain the passages which set out the covenant-law.
5. The best example is perhaps Galatians which, though clearly written in haste, was composed as a forceful presentation of Paul's views. The analysis by H. D. Betz in his Hermeneia Commentary on *Galatians* (Philadelphia: Fortress, 1979), shows how it follows the pattern of a speech, with *exordium, narratio, propositio, probatio* and *exhortatio* enclosed within epistolary prescript and postscript.
6. For Paul, however, the real contrast is between what is 'temporary' and what is 'eternal' – what belongs to this age, and what belongs to the age to come – rather than between the visible and the invisible. See below, pp. 46–7.

Chapter 5

1. The Greek word *euangelion,* normally translated 'gospel', means literally 'good news'.
2. The Hebrew name 'Adam' means 'man'. Paul himself perhaps coined the phrase 'the last Adam', though the idea that Man

(i.e. humanity) will be restored at the end to the condition that Adam had once enjoyed is found in Judaism.

3. 2 Esdras 7:48 (118).
4. The Greek word, *eschaton,* meaning 'end', gives us the word 'eschatology'.
5. There is an interesting parallel in the teaching of Jesus about the Kingdom – or Rule – of God. This is sometimes depicted as future (Matt. 6:10//Luke 11:2), and sometimes referred to as though it were already in some sense here (Matt. 12:28//Luke 11:20).
6. Josephus, *Jewish War,* 7.203 trans H. St. J. Thackeray, Loeb Classical Library (London: Heinemann/Cambridge, MA: Harvard University Press, 1997, first published 1928).

Chapter 6

1. E.g. 1 Sam. 24:6; 2 Sam. 23:1; Ps. 2:2.
2. Pss. Sol. 18:5. 1 QS IX:11; 1 QSa II:11–12. The Psalms of Solomon were probably written in the first century BC. A translation can be found in James H. Charlesworth, ed., *The Old Testament Pseudepigraphia,* Volume 2 (London: Darton, Longman and Todd, 1985). 1 QS (The Community Rule) and 1 QSa (The Messianic Rule) are two of the so-called 'Dead Sea Scrolls'. For the English text, see Geza Vermes, *The Dead Sea Scrolls in English* (London: Penguin, 1995).
3. 1 Kgs. 19:16; Isa. 45:1.
4. Matt. 16:16//Mark 8:29//Luke 9:20; John 1:41.
5. Paul is able to make the analogy because Abraham had believed that God was able to bring a child out of Sarah's apparently dead womb.
6. Rom. 10:9; 1 Cor. 12:3; Phil. 2:11.
7. E.g. Rom. 10:13, quoting Joel 2:32. The quotation appears to refer back to the confession of Jesus as Lord in v. 9. Cf. 1 Cor. 8:6, which builds on Deut. 6:4, but distinguishes between 'God the Father' and 'the Lord Jesus Christ'. In Phil. 2:10, we find Isa. 45:23, a passage originally spoken by the Lord, applied to Christ.
8. Cf. L. Hurtado, *One God, One Lord: Early Christian Devotion and Ancient Jewish Monotheism* (Edinburgh: T. & T. Clark, 2nd edn, 1998).

9. There is much debate among scholars as to whether or not Paul thinks of Christ as God. Some argue that he refers to him as 'God' in Rom. 9:5, but the meaning of that passage is far from clear, as a glance at English translations shows. Richard Bauckham has recently argued that 'New Testament writers clearly and deliberately include Jesus in the unique identity of the God of Israel'. There would be more agreement when he goes on to speak about 'the *revelation* of the divine identity in the human life of Jesus and his cross' (italics mine), since this is an apt summary of what Paul describes in Phil. 2: 5–11, where the one who was in the form of God emptied himself and was obedient to death, so revealing what it meant to be 'in the form of God'. See Richard Bauckham, *God Crucified: Monotheism and Christology in the New Testament* (Carlisle: Paternoster, 1988). Quotations from pp. 77 and 79.
10. The book of Wisdom is one of the books of the Apocrypha. Although the apocryphal books were not part of the Hebrew scriptures, they were included in early Greek translations such as the Septuagint, and also form part of the Roman Catholic canon. Modern versions of the Bible often include the Apocrypha as a separate section.
11. As is done in the 'Florilegium', one of the so-called 'Dead Sea Scrolls' found at Qumran: 4Q Flor. 10–13 (4Q174).
12. So, probably, in the Aramaic Apocalypse (4Q246), another scroll fragment found at Qumran.
13. A 'Life of Apollonius' was written in the third century AD by the Greek philosopher Philostratus.
14. Modern translations often try to avoid offence by removing the masculine language. Here, for example, the NRSV reads 'firstborn within a large family'. On Paul's 'sexist' language, see below.
15. The Aramaic word 'Abba' is said to have been used by Jesus himself in Mark 14:36.
16. Colossians is one of the letters whose Pauline authorship is disputed. Col. 1:13 reminds the Colossians that they have been redeemed by God and transferred into the kingdom of his beloved Son. The phrase 'the Son of God' occurs also in Eph. 4:13, and it is perhaps significant that the context there is somewhat different, since it is highly unlikely that Paul himself wrote Ephesians.

17. Rom. 8:3, 9–17; Gal. 4:4–7. Cf. the similar statements in John 3:17; 10:36; 1 John 4:9, 14.
18. Other passages (e.g. 1 Cor. 8:6; 2 Cor. 8:9; Phil. 2:5–11), as we shall see later, suggest that Paul did think of Christ as pre-existent, although this was controversially denied by J. D. G. Dunn in *Christology in the Making* (London: SCM, 1980, 2nd edn, 1989).
19. Deut. 6:4–5 and Lev. 19:18, quoted in Mark 12:29–31. Cf. Rom. 13:8–10 and Gal. 5:14.

Chapter 7

1. The Greek word *skubala* used here has the meaning 'excrement'.
2. The people attacked here were clearly Jewish. Since there was no reason for non-Christian Jews to attempt to persuade Gentile Christians to become Jews, they were presumably Christians.
3. Rom. 1:5–6; 11:13; 15:15–16; Gal. 4:8; 1 Thess. 1:9.
4. 'Eschatology' means literally 'study of the end', and so refers to beliefs about what would happen when God set things straight at the end of time.
5. E.g. Isa. 40:12–41:13; Amos 1:3–3:2.
6. Joel 2:28–32; cf. Acts 2:16–21.
7. Whether these meals were celebrations of what came to be known as 'the Lord's Supper' or some other type of community meal is debated: probably both took place regularly.
8. Rom. 10:5 and Gal. 3:12, quoting Lev. 18:5.
9. For a detailed discussion of the meaning of Rom. 10:4, see R. Badenas, *Christ the End of the Law: Romans 10: 4 in Pauline Perspective,* JSNT Sup. 10 (Sheffield: JSOT Press, 1985).
10. In Hebrew, the name appears simply as YHWH, since the text contains only consonants. Vowels were added later, but as the sacred name was never pronounced, we do not know what vowels should be used. In modern translations, the form 'Yahweh' is generally used.
11. For similar ideas to those in 2 Corinthians, chs. 3–4 and Colossians 1:15–20, see John 1:1–18 and Hebrews, chs. 1–2.
12. E.g. H. Räisänen, *Paul and the Law,* WUNT 29 (Tübingen: Mohr (Siebeck), 2nd edn, 1987).

Chapter 8

1. Christians trying to explain how this could have happened soon came to interpret Isa. 52:13–53:12 as a prophecy of Jesus' sufferings. Although there has been much discussion about the contemporary Jewish understanding of this passage, there is little evidence to suggest that the suffering it describes was attributed to the Messiah.
2. A similar point is made by the evangelists, who tell the passion story in such a way as to suggest that in declaring Jesus to be worthy of death, the Jewish religious leaders were pronouncing their own condemnation.
3. Rom. 4:24–5. Most commentators assume that the distinction between 'trespasses' and acquittal' (or 'justification') is rhetorical, but there is a logical link between 'trespasses' and 'death' on the one hand, and between 'resurrection' and 'acquittal' on the other. See further, M. D. Hooker, 'Raised for our Acquittal', pp. 283–301 in *Resurrection in the New Testament: Festschrift J. Lambrecht,* ed. R. Bieringer, V. Koperski and B. Lataire (Leuven: Peeters, 2002).
4. These are explored in M. D. Hooker, *From Adam to Christ: Essays on Paul* (Cambridge: CUP, 1990), chapters 5 and 6.
5. E.g. Isa. 46:13; Ps. 98:2, where some modern translators have preferred 'deliverance' or 'vindication'.
6. Qumran is the site in the wilderness, near the Dead Sea, where the so-called 'Dead Sea Scrolls' were found. The Community Document describes the rules governing the life of the sect that lived there.
7. Translation adapted from Geza Vermes, *The Dead Sea Scrolls in English* (London: Penguin, 4th edn, 1995).
8. NRSV, New Revised Standard Version; NIV, New International Version; REB, Revised English Bible; JB, Jerusalem Bible.
9. This was how William Tyndale translated the word; he was influenced at this point by Luther, who translated the word as '*Gnadenstuhl*'. The traditional translation in Heb. 9:5 is 'mercy-seat'.
10. For a detailed examination of the evidence see J. Ziesler, *The meaning of Righteousness in Paul* (Cambridge: CUP, 1972).
11. Most translators make the contrast sharper by translating the Greek word *dikaioma* as 'righteous act'. Paul used it with the meaning 'acquittal' in v. 16, however, and we would expect it to have the

same meaning here. The construction and logic of the Greek are similar to those in Rom. 4:25. See the article referred to in note 3.

12. Cf. a similar interpretation of Adam in 2 Baruch, a Jewish work which was probably written a little after AD 100: 'each of us has become our own Adam' (2 Bar. 54:19).
13. The terms translated 'likeness' and 'form' were intended to denote that Jesus shared fully in human existence.
14. The word Paul uses is in fact 'man', reminding us of the link to Adam.
15. See Philo, a contemporary of Paul's, *Leg. Alleg.* 2: 86. (Trans. F. H. Colson and G. H. Whitaker, Loeb Classical Library. London: Heinemann/Cambridge MA: Harvard University Press, 1929.)

Chapter 9

1. E.g. L. Morris, *The Cross in the Pauline Epistles* (Grand Rapids: Eerdmans, 1965/Exeter: Paternoster, 1976), p. 225.
2. 'Death to sin', also, as we shall see, is something which Christians have to *share* with Christ.
3. For a similar idea, see Col. 1:13–14, which describes how God 'rescued us from the power of darkness and transferred us into the kingdom of his Son, in whom we have redemption, the forgiveness of sins'.
4. Lit. 'being made flesh' – i.e. the taking on of human nature.
5. William Bright, 1824–1901, in the hymn 'And now, O Father, mindful of the love'.
6. *Adv. Haer. V. praef.*
7. Cf. M. D. Hooker, *From Adam to Christ: Essays on Paul* (Cambridge: CUP, 1990), chapters 1–4. The phrase 'interchange' was first used in this sense by R. P. C. Hanson, in connection with what he referred to as the 'interchange between opposites experienced by Christians in 2 Cor. 1:1–7'; see his *II Corinthians* (Torch Commentary) (London: SCM, 1954), pp. 32–5.
8. See above, p. 106.

Chapter 10

1. Also Gal. 3:26, according to one early manuscript.

2. Luther certainly understood the phrase to mean 'faith in Christ'. Earlier translators and commentators are unclear, since they repeat the ambiguity of the Greek.
3. These two ideas are linked. Those who trust in God are themselves faithful – an argument that Paul uses about his own trustworthiness in 2 Cor. 1:17–22.
4. For a summary of arguments about 'the faith of Christ', see M. D. Hooker, *From Adam to Christ: Essays on Paul* (Cambridge: CUP, 1990), ch. 14. For a more detailed discussion, see Richard B. Hays, *The Faith of Christ* (Grand Rapids, MI: Eerdmans, 2nd edn, 2001). Among those who have argued against the view that it refers to Christ's own faithfulness are J. D. G. Dunn; see his *The Theology of Paul the Apostle* (Edinburgh: T. & T. Clark, 1998), pp. 379–85.
5. On the meaning of Phil. 2:5 see Hooker, *From Adam to Christ,* ch. 7.
6. See M. D. Hooker, 'A Partner in the Gospel: Paul's Understanding of His Ministry', in Eugene H. Lovering, Jr., and Jerry L. Sumney, eds., *Theology and Ethics in Paul and His Interpreters,* Essays in Honor of Victor Paul Furnish (Nashville, TN: Abingdon, 1996), pp. 83–100.
7. The Greek word translated 'servants', *diakonoi,* could be used also of servants entrusted with a particular mission – i.e. acting as messengers. Here, Paul and Apollos are clearly acting as the Lord's spokesmen, since they are *diakonoi* 'through whom you believed'. See John N. Collins, *Diakonia* (New York/Oxford: OUP, 1990).
8. Perhaps the most striking example of what this meant for Paul is found in Col. 1:24. Although many scholars are doubtful as to whether or not Paul wrote this letter, it certainly develops his theology in ways that are compatible with the rest of his thought. In this verse, Paul (if he is the author) rejoices in his suffering 'for your sake', and claims to be completing 'what is lacking in Christ's sufferings in my flesh for the sake of his body, that is the church'. The idea that there might be something lacking in Christ's sufferings has often puzzled commentators, for it is clear elsewhere that Paul does not believe that there is anything lacking in those sufferings. But what *may* be lacking is apparently 'Christ's sufferings in my flesh' – i.e. the extent to which Paul has thus far shared in those sufferings. His aim is to complete what he has been called to do and to endure for the

sake of Christ's body, the Church. See further W. F. Flemington, 'On the interpretation of Colossians 1: 24', in William Horbury and Brian McNeil, eds., *Suffering and Martyrdom in the New Testament* (Cambridge: CUP, 1981), pp. 84–90.

9. Even the temple 'grows', 1 Cor. 3:10–15.
10. See above, n. 7. The *diakonoi* may have been as much concerned with the ministry of evangelism as with serving 'at tables' (Acts 6: 1–6).
11. In Phoebe's case, however, she is perhaps referred to as a *diakonos* because she comes to Rome from Cenchreae as the authorized spokeswoman of the church there.
12. Cf. also Eph. 5:22–6:9.

Chapter 11

1. 'Nomism' from Greek *nomos,* 'law'. The term 'covenantal nomism' was first used by E. P. Sanders. See *Paul and Palestinian Judaism* (London: SCM, 1977).
2. Although Jewish prophets were not unknown (Anna is mentioned in Luke 2:36–8), they would have been rare.
3. This has been disputed, and there is in fact no clear contemporary evidence to prove it. Nevertheless, the earliest records and archaeological evidence that we have support this view, and the practice seems to go back to worship in the Temple, where there was a separate 'Court of Women'. Women were clearly included in Jewish worship, but were separated from men. For a full discussion of the question, see William Horbury, 'Women in the Synagogue', pp. 358–401 in *The Cambridge History of Judaism,* Volume 3, eds. William Horbury, W. D. Davies and John Sturdy (Cambridge: CUP, 1999).
4. Paul gives no instructions about whether or not men and women should sit separately in Christian worship. In the third century AD, however, segregation was apparently common.
5. See Gerd Theissen, *The Social Setting of Pauline Christianity* (Edinburgh: T. & T. Clark, 1982), pp. 145–74.
6. Sermon on the Mount IV. 1.1 (John Wesley's *Fourty-four Sermons,* Sermon XIX).

7. There is some textual evidence to suggest that vv. 34–5 are a later addition to the letter. Although they are found in all our manuscripts, they occur after v. 40 in a few of them, and it has been argued that the verses were originally a marginal gloss, which subsequently made its way into the text. In that case, the comment would have been made by someone who supported the view expressed in 1 Tim. 2:11–12.
8. 1 Cor. 7:10–11; 9:14. There are no other explicit references. Among those who have argued for the influence of Jesus' teaching on Paul are David Wenham, in *Paul: Follower of Jesus or Founder of Christianity?* (Grand Rapids, MI/Cambridge: Eerdmans, 1995).

Chapter 12

1. Examples are Daniel in the Old Testament, and I Enoch.
2. Cf. Joel 2:1; Zeph. 1:14–16.
3. Compare the way in which Old Testament prophets declared 'the word of the Lord', e.g. Hos. 4:1; Amos 1:3.
4. Although Matt. 24:31, which is suggested by some scholars to be a parallel, refers to the coming of the Son of man, the trumpet call and the gathering of the elect, it makes no mention of the resurrection of the dead, which is the point that Paul is emphasizing in 1 Thessalonians.
5. The verb is the familiar *dikaioo* (to 'right'). The context here is clearly that of a court of law, and for God to 'right' men and women presumably means that he acquits them. The language echoes that of Isa. 50:8.

Epilogue

1. Other Christians may not have respected Paul's writings so highly. The letter of James is thought by some to be attacking Paul's teaching about the importance of faith for salvation. See, for example, James 2:14–26, which appears to dispute Paul's central teaching in Romans. What James is advocating, however, when he insists on the necessity for 'works', is what Paul referred to as 'the obedience of faith'. It is possible that what James is attacking here is a garbled report or misunderstanding of Paul's teaching.

2. See J. M. G. Barclay, *Colossians and Philemon* (Sheffield: Sheffield Academic Press, 1997), pp. 113–26.
3. In Gal. 3:28, Paul affirms that in the Christian community Jews and Gentiles, slaves and free, male and female, all have equal status before God. Nevertheless, insisting on one's 'rights' can conflict with the demands of Christian love; cf. 1 Cor. 6:1–8; chs. 8–9.
4. This interpretation was grossly unfair to Judaism, which was founded on God's grace in saving Israel. E. P. Sanders, *Paul and Palestinian Judaism* (London: SCM, 1977), stressed this fact, and so introduced what is commonly known as 'The new perspective on Paul'. The law was given within the context of God's covenant with Israel, which was based on his saving grace; hence Sanders' understanding of Judaism as 'covenantal nomism'. Sanders' work led to a proliferation of scholarly writings about Paul and the law. Among those in broad agreement with his approach we may mention J. D. G. Dunn who, however, has stressed that Paul's criticism is basically about relying on 'the works of the law', and who suggests that this is because they were seen as 'identity markers', separating Israel from the Gentiles, and so the cause of boasting. See his *Jesus, Paul and the Law* (Louisville, KY: Westminster/John Knox, 1990), pp. 183–264, and *The Theology of Paul the Apostle* (Edinburgh: T.& T. Clark, 1998), pp. 128–61, 354–66.
5. See, e.g. R. Bultmann, *Theology of the New Testament,* vol. 1 English translation (London: SCM, 1952).
6. See, e.g. the influential book by W. D. Davies, *Paul and Rabbinic Judaism* (London: SPCK, 1948, 2nd edn, 1955).
7. It can be safely said that this is now how the majority of Pauline scholars see him.
8. The 'Lutheran' interpretation is represented by Ernst Käsemann, e.g. in *Perspectives on Paul,* English translation (London: SCM, 1971), pp. 60–101.
9. Albert Schweitzer, *The Mysticism of Paul the Apostle,* English translation (London: A. & C. Black, 1931, 2nd edn, 1953).
10. K. Stendahl, *Paul Among Jews and Gentiles* (London: SCM, 1977), pp. 23–40.
11. See, e.g. the work of B. J. Malina, *The New Testament World: Insights from Cultural Anthropology* (Louisville, KY: Westminster/John Knox

Press, 3rd edn, 2001). He argues, for example, that terms such as 'honour' and 'shame', which have one set of meanings today, would have conveyed significantly different meanings to a first-century reader.

12. E.g. G. Theissen, *The Social Setting of Pauline Christianity* (Edinburgh: T. & T. Clark, 1982); W. A. Meeks, *The First Urban Christians* (New Haven & London: Yale University Press, 1983).
13. This analyses Paul's letters in the light of the conventions adopted in ancient rhetoric. See, e.g. H. D. Betz, *Galatians: A Commentary on Paul's Letter to the Churches in Galatia* (Philadelphia: Fortress, 1979).
14. For analysis and discussion of this approach, see *Narrative Dynamics in Paul: A Critical Assessment,* ed. B. W. Longenecker (Louisville, KY: Westminster/John Knox Press, 2002).
15. See Elizabeth Schlüssler Fiorenza, *In Memory of Her* (London: SCM, 1983); Brendan Byrne, *Paul and the Christian Woman* (Homebush, NSW: St. Paul Publications, 1988). The danger with feminist criticism, however, is that it sometimes fails to see Paul in his own context, and judges him against the insights of the modern world.
16. In the Fourth Gospel, unlike the first three, the teaching attributed to Jesus is about his own role and his relationship with his Father. A comparison with the other gospels, however, shows that this is not his own teaching, but that of others about him.

Bibliography

An asterisk (*) before an entry indicates an introductory work.

General

*Barrett, C. K., *Paul: An Introduction to His Thought,* London: Geoffrey Chapman, 1994.

Becker, Jürgen, *Paul: Apostle to the Gentiles,* Louisville, KY: Westminster/John Knox, 1993.

Dunn, James D. G., *The Theology of Paul the Apostle,* Edinburgh: T. & T. Clark, 1998.

*Hooker, M. D., *Pauline Pieces,* London: Epworth, 1979 (= *A Preface to Paul,* New York: OUP, 1980).

Hooker, Morna D., *From Adam to Christ: Essays on Paul,* Cambridge: CUP, 1990.

Sanders, E. P., *Paul and Palestinian Judaism,* Philadelphia: Fortress/London: SCM, 1977.

*Sanders, E. P., *Paul,* Oxford and New York: OUP, 1991.

Stendahl, Krister, *Paul Among Jews and Gentiles,* London: SCM, 1977.

*Wright, Tom, *What Saint Paul Really Said,* Oxford: Lion, 1997.

*Ziesler, John, *Pauline Christianity,* rev. edn, Oxford and New York: OUP, 1990.

Dictionary of Paul and His Letters, eds Gerald F. Hawthorne, Ralph P. Martin, Daniel G. Reid, Leicester: InterVarsity Press, 1993.

Chapter 2

Hengel, Martin, *The Pre-Christian Paul,* London: SCM/Philadelphia: TPI, 1992.

Jewett, Robert, *Dating Paul's Life,* London: SCM, 1979.

Knox, John, *Chapters in a Life of Paul,* New York: Abingdon-Cokesbury, 1950/London: A. & C. Black, 1954.

Murphy-O'Connor, Jerome, *Paul: A Critical Life,* Oxford and New York: OUP, 1997.

Witherington, Ben III, *The Paul Quest: The Renewed Search for the Jew of Tarsus,* Leicester: IVP, 1998.

Chapter 4

Wallace, Richard, and Williams, Wynne, *The Three Worlds of Paul of Tarsus,* London/New York: Routledge, 1998.

Chapter 6

Dunn, James D. G., *Christology in the Making,* London: SCM, 1980.

Hengel, Martin, *The Son of God,* London: SCM, 1976.

Moule, C. F. D., *The Origin of Christology,* Cambridge: CUP, 1977.

*Tuckett, Christopher M., *Christology and the New Testament,* Edinburgh: University Press, 2001.

Chapter 7

*Hooker, Morna D., *Continuity and Discontinuity,* London: Epworth, 1986.

*Koperski, Veronica, *What are they Saying about Paul and the Law?* New York: Paulist Press, 2001.

Westerholm, Stephen, *Israel's Law and the Church's Faith: Paul and His Recent Interpreters,* Grand Rapids, MI: Eerdmans, 1988.

Wright, N. T., *The Climax of the Covenant,* Edinburgh: T. & T. Clark, 1991.

Chapter 8

Best, E., *One Body in Christ,* London: SPCK, 1955.

Schweitzer, Albert, *The Mysticism of Paul the Apostle,* London: A. & C. Black, 2nd edn, 1953.

Chapter 9

Grayston, K., *Dying We Live,* London: Darton, Longman and Todd, 1990.
*Hooker, M. D., *Not Ashamed of the Gospel,* Carlisle: Paternoster, 1994/ Grand Rapids, MI: Eerdmans, 1995.

Chapter 10

Gorman, Michael J., *Cruciformity; Paul's Narrative Spirituality of the Cross,* Grand Rapids, MI/Cambridge: Eerdmans, 2001.
Hays, Richard B., *The Faith of Jesus Christ: The Narrative Substructure of Galatians 3:1–4:11,* Grand Rapids MI/Cambridge: Eerdmans, 2nd edn, 2002.

Chapter 11

*Furnish, Victor Paul, *Jesus According to Paul,* Cambridge: CUP, 1993.
*Furnish, Victor Paul, *The Moral Teaching of Paul,* Nashville TN: Abingdon, 1979.
Furnish, Victor Paul, *Theology and Ethics in Paul,* Nashville TN/New York: Abingdon, 1968.

Chapter 12

Lincoln, Andrew T., *Paradise Now and Not Yet,* Cambridge: CUP, 1981.

Epilogue

*Horrell, David, *An Introduction to the Study of Paul,* London/New York: Continuum, 2000.

Index

Index of citations